歐盟貿易政策新趨勢

The New Trend of the EU Trade Policy

U0081933

陳麗娟 主編

淡江大學出版中心

CONTENTS

i

序言

　　歐盟歷經一甲子以上的統合發展，至今仍屹立不搖，歐盟結合了 28 個會員國的經濟實力，且已經成為全球最大的經濟實體，在國際經貿社會舉足輕重，並扮演領頭羊的角色。WTO 是歐盟與台灣經貿往來重要的平台，歐盟在 WTO 中扮演一個領航的角色，是全球最大的經濟體，歐盟在 WTO 有很大的影響力，例如目前歐盟的『綠色經濟』、『綠色產業』的倡議，已經反映在 2012 年的 GPA『綠色政府採購』，因此歐盟的技術標準與規則逐漸成為 WTO 的規範，歐盟實際上積極參與全球治理，而影響著全球的產業政策。

　　歐盟莫內講座（Jean Monnet Chair）計畫贊助，由莫內講座教授陳麗娟博士主辦『歐盟貿易政策新趨勢國際研討會』，以期國內產官學對於歐盟貿易政策新趨勢之認識與因應。本書集結 7 篇論文，立論精闢，見解獨到，希冀將研討會的成果與社會大眾分享，以期產官學各界可以進一步瞭解歐盟貿易政策之新趨勢。

淡江大學歐洲聯盟研究中心主任
莫內講座教授
陳麗娟
2016.05.18 於淡水

歐盟貿易政策新趨勢

陳麗娟
淡江大學歐洲研究所教授
莫內講座教授
德國慕尼黑大學法學博士

壹、前言：研究動機與目的

歐盟的人口總數已經超過美國和俄羅斯的總和，已經是全球最大且最重要的經濟與貿易實體之一，並創造全球四分之一的財富，也是全球最大的援助貧窮落後國家的經濟實體，2002 年啟用單一貨幣歐元（Euro），而歐元也成為國際金融市場上僅次於美元的第二個重要貨幣。2008 年全球金融海嘯後，歐盟體認到貿易是促進經濟成長與創造就業的重要方法，因此歐盟鼓吹在全球化下促進經濟利益，亦希望在 WTO 多邊的貿易架構下，可以增加與第三國的貿易關係，以期可以儘速致力於經濟復甦，走出經濟谷底。

　　本文探討歐盟貿易政策的新趨勢，首先闡述歐盟在國際社會的全球角色（global actor），特別是在 WTO 的架構下，歐盟扮演著領導的角色。2008 年全球金融海嘯後，接著引發歐債風暴，歐盟體認到貿易是促進經濟成長與創造就業的發動機。共同貿易政策包羅萬象，2015 年 10 月時，歐盟執委會公布了一份文件『貿易包羅萬象：邁向更有責任的貿易與投資政策』，揭示了歐盟貿易政策的新趨勢。因此，以此一文件為主，分析歐盟貿易政策新趨勢的詳細內容，以期進一步瞭解歐盟貿易政策的新趨勢。

貳、歐盟在國際社會的地位

一、歐盟統合的現況

第二次世界大戰結束後，國際社會有了很大的轉變，國際政治舞台由歐洲大陸移往美國，也因而促使西歐各國的緊密合作與和平相處，在逆境中求生存，才有歐洲煤鋼共同體、歐洲經濟共同體與歐洲原子能共同體的誕生，而隨著時間的推移演進逐步發展，使歐盟成為歐洲大陸的一個單一貿易實體與經濟實體，也是全球區域統合的典範。

在建立歐盟基礎條約法律規範的基礎上，在經濟統合的軌跡上，歐盟由關稅同盟開始、逐步完成單一市場進而邁向貨幣暨經濟同盟[1]，進而逐步發展成為一個政治同盟，目前已經囊括了 28 個會員國[2]，而會員國並沒有因為成為歐盟的一員，而喪失其在國際社會的主權地位，而是結合了 28 個會員國的實力，使得歐盟成為國際社會的一個政治實體與積極的扮演全球角色。

目前歐盟有超過五億人口，在國際金融市場上，歐元已經成為第二個重要的國際貨幣，是全球第二大的儲備貨幣。目前使用歐元的國家有荷蘭、比利時、盧森堡、德國、法國、義大利、西班牙、葡萄牙、奧地利、芬蘭、愛爾蘭、希臘、賽浦路斯、馬爾它、斯洛維尼亞、斯洛伐克、愛沙尼亞、拉脫維亞，立陶宛亦於 2015 年 1 月 1 日開始使用歐元，目前共有 19 個會員國使用歐元，統稱為歐元區（Euro Area）。

歐元區已經形成一個經濟實體，經濟實力不容忽視。全球金融海嘯

---

[1] 經濟暨貨幣同盟主要的要素，為協調會員國的經濟政策、實施單一貨幣、與建立歐洲中央銀行制度。自 1999 年 1 月 1 日起，位於德國法蘭克福的歐洲中央銀行開始肩負起制訂歐元區（Euro Area）貨幣政策的任務。創立歐元區與設立一個新的超國家組織–歐洲中央銀行，經濟暨貨幣同盟使得歐洲統合邁向一個新的里程碑。

[2] 六個創始會員國：德國、法國、義大利、荷蘭、比利時、盧森堡；第一次擴大 1973 年英國、丹麥與愛爾蘭加入；第二次擴大 1981 年增加希臘；第三次擴大：1986 年西班牙與葡萄牙加入；第四次擴大：1995 年奧地利、瑞典與芬蘭加入；第五次擴大：2004 年增加了賽浦路斯、波蘭、捷克共和國、匈牙利、立陶宛、愛沙尼亞、拉脫維亞、斯洛伐克共和國、斯洛維尼亞與馬爾它；2007 年保加利亞與羅馬尼亞亦成為會員國；2013 年 7 月 1 日克羅埃西亞加入歐盟。

與接續的歐債風暴曝露了歐洲金融市場的缺陷，因此歐盟與全體會員國進行了一系列的金融改革，然而在歐洲單一金融市場的概念下，應如何有效掌控金融市場的良性運作，仍然是一個嚴峻的挑戰。總而言之，自2008 年以來，全球經濟接連在金融風暴、歐債風暴的漩渦中持續衰退，促使歐盟發展新的經濟治理（Economic Governance）模式。

2010 年 6 月，歐洲高峰會議公布『歐洲 2020 策略』（Europe 2020 Strategy）[3] 取代了原來的里斯本策略（Lisbon Strategy）[4]，計畫在 2011 年至 2020 年進行致力於 3 個優先的目標，即智慧成長、永續成長與融合成長，以發展以知識和創新為基礎的產業、促進愛惜能源、更環保與有競爭力的產業、以及促進有高就業、打造社會和領域結合的產業。『歐洲 2020 策略』為歐盟新的政策策略，以致力於提高就業、生產力與社會融合。在全球化、氣候變遷與人口老化的現實環境下，歐盟經歷這些現象所產生的衝擊，再加上 2008 年以來的金融危機與經濟衰退，執委會更體認到經濟繁榮與創造就業應配合一系列的改革措施，才能確保未來 10 年歐盟的永續發展。

二、歐盟的全球角色

成立於 1995 年的 WTO，是最重要的國際經貿組織，歐盟與其全體會員國同時都是 WTO 的正式會員國，明確的規範歐盟與 WTO 間的法律關係，WTO 的規定同時對歐盟與其全體會員國有法律拘束力。 WTO 的規範已經被承認是歐盟法律制度的一部份，同時已經納入許多 WTO 會員國的國內法中。在 WTO 重要的會議中，歐盟的個別會員國協調其立場與意見，而由歐盟的執行委員會單獨地為全體會員國的利益發言、代表一個共同的立場。因此，在實務上，歐盟成為與其他 WTO 會員國主要的談判夥伴。

全球化的要求和國際經濟規範自由化的趨勢，主要都在 WTO 彰

---

[3]　COM (2010) 2020 final.

[4]　2000 年 3 月 23/24 日，在里斯本舉行歐洲高峰會議的特別會議，期待歐洲合作邁入一個新階段，在此次的歐洲高峰會議訂下一個目標，即至 2010 年止應使歐盟成為一個以知識為基礎、全球最有競爭力與最有活力的經濟區，提出了所謂的里斯本策略。COM (2001) 641 final.

顯出來，這些現象促使歐盟的貿易政策進一步的擴張至其他領域的經濟活動。在 1992 年完成單一市場後，亦循著此一發展趨勢，也就是要促成跨越商品交易的範圍而形成共同的對外經濟政策。阿姆斯特丹條約與尼斯條約邁出了第一步，建立了一個整合的對外貿易和經濟政策；2006年時，執行委員會提出一個名為『在全球化世界有競爭力的歐洲』（Ein Wettbewerbsfähiges Europa in einer Globalen Welt）的函示[5]，亦提出歐盟對外角色的議題，以期補充里斯本策略。2009 年 12 月生效的里斯本條約試圖填補剩下的鴻溝與簡化在共同貿易政策的規則。也就是歐盟以政治團結與經濟實力面對全球化的挑戰，以期使歐盟成為全球化世界的新角色，歐盟也必須立即行動以利用全球化的機會。

里斯本條約確立了歐洲聯盟的國際法律人格，歐洲聯盟條約第 1 條第 3 項明文規定，聯盟的基礎為本條約與歐洲聯盟運作條約；此二條約在法律上位階相同。歐洲聯盟取代歐洲共同體，歐洲聯盟是歐洲共同體法律上的繼承者。依據此一規定，歐洲聯盟條約與歐洲聯盟運作方式條約不僅有相同的憲法位階，而且歐洲聯盟是歐洲共同體的繼承者[6]，歐洲聯盟成為國際法上的主體，享有國際法律人格。

隨著 1995 年 WTO 的設立與 1990 年代國際經濟法的蓬勃發展，里斯本條約將 WTO 架構下的三大領域，即商品貿易、服務業貿易、與貿易有關的智慧財產權保護明文規定完全屬於歐盟的專屬職權[7]，也就是會員國不得在這些範圍締結國際法上的協定。由於共同貿易政策不再區分商品貿易、服務貿易、涉及智慧財產的貿易，而里斯本條約也將社會、衛生、教育和文化服務納入共同貿易政策的職權範圍，授與歐盟專屬的職權參與 WTO，因而能參與 WTO 修訂各項協定的談判。也就是在 WTO 架構下，歐盟成為唯一的發言人，由歐盟以一致的聲音（one voice）對外發言，全體會員國不得再就貿易議題對外發言。

里斯本條約改革了共同貿易政策，並且使歐盟的對外關係進入一

---

[5]　COM (2006) 567 final.

[6]　Albrecht Weber, Vom Verfassungsvertrag zum Vertrag von Lissabon, EuZW 2008, S.7.

[7]　C. Herrmann/H. G. Krenzler/R. Streinz (Hrsg.)，*Der Vertrag von Lissabon zur Reform der Europäischen Union*, 2008, S.170.

個新紀元，要致力於發展連貫、有效率與包羅萬象的貿易政策。里斯本條約擴大了共同貿易政策的適用範圍，與 WTO 架構的內容相同，不再區分商品貿易、服務貿易、涉及智慧財產的貿易，顯然里斯本條約不再侷限於共同貿易政策傳統的特徵，而是擴大到共同貿易政策其他的經濟活動。里斯本條約要保證在一個全球化的世界有效率的適用共同貿易政策，以一個簡化且明確的方式，由歐盟專屬的行使對第三國的共同貿易政策。因此，加強歐盟在對外關係與國際貿易事務的行為能力，特別是在對外貿易關係上完全取代全體會員國，猶如一個國家出現在國際社會，有助於多邊貿易談判更有效率的進行。一方面要達成內部經濟統合的目標，另一方面要提高歐盟在國際社會的競爭力。WTO 的杜哈回合（Doha Round）即是由歐盟單獨全權的參與談判，而成為真正的單一經濟區。總而言之，里斯本條約鞏固了歐盟的全球角色，歐盟也更積極的參與全球經濟治理。

三、全球金融海嘯後『經濟新霸權』的崛起

冷戰結束後，世界的政治和經濟權力分配起了根本的變化，全球化使各國的經濟更加緊密的結合在一起，跨國的資金流通與跨國公司的蓬勃發展，也促使國際投資增加。美國、中國與歐盟形成一個新的三角關係，特別是藉由更好的雙邊協定與新興市場維持良好的經濟、夥伴與投資保護的關係[8]。在這種競爭與夥伴關係中，歐盟必須在對外貿易關係上確保歐洲的成長與繁榮，因此在全球的舞台上，歐盟本身必須保持有效率的行為能力[9]。歐盟的全體會員國相互保障和平、發展及合作、並實現單一市場的目標，在歐洲的統合進程進一步邁向在全球的政治與經濟自主的地位[10]。

　　歐盟已經成為國際社會重要的對話夥伴，全球化的國際經貿發展促

---

[8]　Marc Bungenberg, Auβenbeziehungen und Auβenhandelspolirik, EuR 2009, Beiheft 1, S.195.

[9]　P. Schiffauer, Zum Verfassungszustand der europäischen Union nach Unterzeichnung des Vertrags von Lissabon, EUGRZ 2008, S.9.

[10]　K. Hänsch, Ende gut – alles gut? Anmerkungen zum Reformvertrag, Integration 4/2007, S.499ff.

成跨國企業的蓬勃發展，亦衍生出新的投資保護議題。自 2001 年杜哈回合以來，由於已開發國家、新興經濟體、開發中國家與低度開發國家對於全球經貿議題意見紛歧，終於在 2013 年 12 月中旬達成所謂的『峇里套案』（Bali Package），而成為新的經貿規則。冗長的杜哈回合談判使得 WTO 的多邊貿易體制受到嚴峻的挑戰，區域貿易協定與雙邊自由貿易協定又孕運而生，逐漸成為全球治理的重要機制。除了與美國維持定期的跨大西洋經濟對話與積極諮商 TTIP（跨大西洋貿易暨投資夥伴協定）的議題外，歐盟亦與中國維持良好的對話機制，以期可以『左右逢緣』，以協助歐洲企業開發新的商機與拓展出口市場。

貿易政策是『歐洲 2020 策略』的核心要素，貿易是促進經濟繁榮的發動機[11]，貿易已經是歐盟作為實現『歐洲 2020 策略』的重要手段。同時，歐盟愈來愈重視投資保護議題，歐盟將投資保護作為簽訂雙邊協定的新議題。投資與貿易相互依賴，又互為補充，投資直接影響貿易、工作機會與資金流動。投資已經成為歐盟共同貿易政策的一部分，由於共同貿易政策屬於歐盟的專屬職權，因此執委會亦就投資立法，2010年執委會在一個名為『貿易包羅萬象：邁向廣泛的歐洲國際投資政策』（Trade for all: Towards a comprehensive European international investment policy）的函示[12]中描繪歐盟未來的投資政策，表明投資政策致力於『歐洲 2020 策略』智慧、永續與融合成長之目標。顯見，投資也成為歐盟在全球治理上重要的方法。

歐盟的投資政策係致力於給予歐盟的投資人與投資更大的市場進入、法律安定性、一個穩定、可預期、公平合適當規範的環境。目前執委會在談判自由貿易協定時，均會與貿易夥伴討論投資保護，例如與加拿大、印度、新加坡等的自由貿易協定談判均納入投資保護的議題，而歐盟亦積極的參與國際組織（例如 OECD、UNCTAD[13]、WTO、G8[14]、

---

[11] European Commission staff working document "Trade as a driver of prosperity", SEC (2010) 1269.

[12] COM (2010) 343 final.

[13] 即聯合國貿易暨發展委員會。

[14] G8 為八大工業國，即日本、加拿大、美國、德國、法國、英國、義大利與俄羅斯，定期商討當下的重要經貿議題。

IMF）的國際投資規則擬定。由於有將近 1200 個由會員國簽署的雙邊投資協定，因此歐盟逐步的實施廣泛的投資政策，以取代這些原來由會員國與第三國簽署的投資協定。2012 年公布第 1219 號規章 [15] 即規範至歐盟的投資協定生效時止，這些由會員國與第三國簽署的雙邊投資協定享有法律保障，同時並允許執委會授權會員國與第三國開始正式的談判以在特定條件下修改或締結雙邊投資協定。

整體而言，歐盟投資政策的目標為：

1. 致力於長期投資，以創造穩定的就業與成長；
2. 改善市場進入與確保外國投資享有國民待遇；
3. 以明確的規範架構促進程序透明；
4. 確保投資地主國與母國完全保有規範國內領域的權利；
5. 自由移轉支付及與投資有關的資金流動，僅在例外情形才得採取防衛措施；
6. 促進與投資有關的人員流通。

自 2009 年 12 月里斯本條約生效時起，歐盟對於投資保護協定亦享有職權，歐盟可以在貿易與投資協定中制訂一套單一的投資保護規則，可以避免在會員國間因不同的保護規則而造成法律規避的現象，此一規定有利於歐盟與全體會員國建立一個統一的投資保護制度，因此歐盟並規範投資保護規定與投資人地主國爭端解決機制；自 2010 年起，執委會即開始著手明確化與改善國際投資保護制度 [16]。

執委會闡明在貿易協定內包含投資保護條款的理由，主要是投資是影響經濟成長與就業的重要因素，貿易與投資是歐盟經濟發展的動力，特別是投資可以創造與維持商機及工作機會，透過投資行為，企業可以形塑全球的價值鏈，增加在現代國際經濟的影響力，不僅創造新的貿易機會，而且創造加值的就業機會與增加收入。因此，執委會認為應在貿易協定中鼓勵投資，以便為歐洲企業創造投資於全球的契機 [17]。

---

[15] OJ 2012 L 351/40.

[16] http://eropa.eu/rapid/press-release_IP-14-56_en.htm, last visited 2014/06/11.

[17] European Commission, *Investment Protection and Investor-to-State Dispute Settlement in EU Agreements*, November 2013, pp.3-4.

目前全體會員國已經簽署了超過 1400 個投資保護協定 [18]，由於歐盟在國際經貿社會已經佔有舉足輕重的地位，因此歐盟在國際社會主導著投資保護協定的內容，以期向其貿易夥伴要求更清楚與更好的保護標準。當然在多邊層次，特別是聯合國國際貿易法（United Nations on International Trade Law；簡稱 UNCITRAL）歐盟亦施展其影響力，致力於創設新的程序透明原則；另外，歐盟主要的作法還是藉由與第三國締結雙邊協定規範投資保護，歐盟正逐步以雙邊的自由貿易協定落實其投資保護規則。

總而言之，歐盟所有的自由貿易協定均明確的規定締約國的規範權（right to regulate）與致力於正當的公共政策目標，例如社會、環保、安全、公共衛生與安全、以及促進與保護文化多樣性等 [19]。由歐盟締結含有投資保護的貿易協定，將取代原來會員國簽署的雙邊投資協定，例如執委會與中國及緬甸談判投資協定亦包含投資保護、與加拿大、印度、日本、摩洛哥、新加坡、泰國、越南與美國進行自由貿易協定談判，亦包含投資保護在內。由此可見，貿易與投資已經是緊密結合在一起，而在歐盟新一代的自由貿易協定更是涵蓋投資議題，在經濟統合更進一步深化後，歐盟已經以『經濟新霸權』之姿，站上全球經貿舞台。

參、歐盟貿易政策新趨勢

2015 年 10 月，執委會公布了一個貿易政策新趨勢的文件 [20]，明確的表明歐盟要以貿易作為手段，以促進對消費者、勞工與小企業的實際經濟成效，同時歐盟仍持續以開放的市場促進全球的議題，例如維護人權與永續發展、在歐盟境內高品質的安全、環境法規與公共服務。貿易政策扮演一個更重要的角色，將肩負更多的責任，也就是貿易政策應更有效率、更透明，不僅反應歐盟的利益，同時更應反應歐盟的價值。

---

[18] European Commission, *Investment Protection and Investor-to-State Dispute Settlement in EU Agreements*, November 2013, p.1.

[19] European Commission, *Investment Protection and Investor-to-State Dispute Settlement in EU Agreements*, November 2013, p.7.

[20] European Commission, *Trade for all*, 2015 Brussels.

這份文件包括五個部分，即

1. 貿易與投資是成長與創造就業強而有力的發動機；
2. 有效率的政策可以掌握新的經濟現狀與具體落實各項目標；
3. 更透明的貿易與投資政策；
4. 貿易與投資政策應以價值為基礎；
5. 預期的談判計畫應形成全球化治理。

一、文件提出背景

在經歷全球金融海嘯的經濟衰退後，歐盟目前最大的挑戰就是鼓勵就業、成長與投資。因此執委會小以『就業、成長與投資』做為其政策方針的首要目標，貿易是促進經濟、卻又不會造成國家財政負擔的一個重要手段，同時貿易也是會員國結構改革與歐盟投資計畫[21] 的一部分。

歐盟將運用貿易與投資政策，以致力於達成目標，同時使企業、消費者與勞工從中獲利。歐盟是全球商品及服務最大的出口者與進口者、最大的外國直接投資者與最重要的外國直接投資目的地，因而使歐盟成為約 80 個國家最大的貿易夥伴與約 40 個國家的第二大最重要夥伴。藉由貿易，歐盟不僅使歐盟人民受惠，亦嘉惠其他國家的人民[22]。

目前的經濟制度以全球化與數位化為核心，依據國際的價值鏈，而有許多國家參與想法、設計與製造。因此，歐盟的貿易與投資政策亦必須考量其他國家，尤其是目前的貿易不同於傳統的交易，愈來愈多也包含人員的移動與資訊交流，而不是只是跨國的商品交易，因此歐盟的貿易政策亦必須順應時代的變化而做調整。

有效率的貿易政策應推動歐盟的發展與更廣泛的對外政策，對外政策與對內政策應相互支援。貿易政策結合發展合作，有助於開發中國家的成長，歐盟將持續在貿易政策中，致力於永續發展的承諾、致力於聯合國 2030 年永續發展的全球永續發展目標[23]。

貿易政策提高歐盟單一市場的作用，而使單一市場的規則與全球

---

[21] COM (2014) 903 final.

[22] European Commission, *Trade for all*, 2015 Brussels, p.7.

[23] United Nations, Transforming our World – The 2030 Agenda for Sustainable Development.

締結或正在談判洽簽雙邊的自由貿易協定[33]。目前雙邊自由貿易協定已經涵蓋歐盟三分之一的貿易,一旦全部的雙邊自由貿易協定談判完成,將涵蓋歐盟三分之二的貿易,雙邊自由貿易協定可以說是全球最重要的貿易議題。歐盟與韓國的自由貿易協定是新一代協定(new generation agreement)的最佳範例,雙方在五年內降低了 99% 的關稅與廢除非關稅的貿易障礙,歐盟的出口增加,歐盟長期的貿易赤字已經轉為盈餘,而歐盟自韓國的進口亦由 9% 增加到 13%[34]。

有利的貿易政策,同時應有國內的改革相互支援,也就是進行結構改革、更少的繁文褥節、更容易取得融資與更多的基礎設施投資、專業人才與研究發展,都有助於提升歐盟從開放市場受惠的能力。在歐盟層級,歐盟的投資計畫亦與這些改革配合,將使歐洲企業,特別是中小企業,更有競爭力;會員國亦進行結構的改革,有助於貿易的績效。歐洲學期(European Semester)是最重要的供去,以最大化貿易與國內政策的配套措施[35]。

歐盟的貿易政策應加強歐盟在全球供應鏈的地位,應支援許多的經濟活動,例如零組件與成品製造、服務、研究、設計與行銷、組裝、分配與維修[36]。順應現實的國際經貿環境,歐盟的貿易政策已經從傳統的關稅擴大到很多重要的議題,例如政府採購、競爭、補貼、衛生與檢疫障礙等。以政府採購為例,全球 GDP 的 15% 至 20% 運用於公共支出,基礎設施投資、其他新興國家及已開發國家的政府採購在未來是推動經濟成長的重要方法。歐盟已經是一個整合且開放的市場,但歐盟企業在海外卻面臨差別待遇與不同的限制,因此應確保市場進入的平順運作,歐盟則是藉由自由貿易協定與談判新成員加入 WTO 的政府採購協定[37]。

同時,貿易政策亦應找出更多的議題,以確保歐盟在全球價值鏈的

---

[33] 參閱 http://trade.ec.europa.eu/doclib/docs/2006/december/tradoc_118238.pdf.

[34] European Commission, *Trade for all*, 2015 Brussels, p.9.

[35] European Commission, *Trade for all*, 2015 Brussels, p.9.

[36] European Commission, *Trade for all*, 2015 Brussels, p.10.

[37] European Commission, *Trade for all*, 2015 Brussels, p.10.

地位，因此應促進服務貿易、數位貿易、支持專業人員的移動、指出法規不完備的情形、確保取得原料、保護創新與確保快速的海關管理。貿易協定應支援促進透明化的國際標準與好的治理[38]。

（一）促進服務貿易

服務業佔歐盟 GDP 的 70%，在國際貿易中，服務貿易愈來愈重要，服務貿易成為歐盟貿易政策的優先項目，歐盟是 WTO 複邊的服務貿易協定（Trade in Service Agreement；簡稱 TiSA）的 23 個締約國[39]之一，積極鼓吹應致力於服務自由化與制定規則。歐盟對於公共服務，例如供水、教育、衛生與社會服務，並不會要求會員國政府民營化任何公共服務，也不會阻止會員國政府擴大給社會大眾的服務範圍[40]。

（二）促進數位貿易

數位革命消除了國與國間地理和距離的障礙，在全球，數位革命也對經濟及社會帶來巨大的衝擊，就貿易而言，數位意涵著新的機會，尤其是對歐盟的中小企業與消費者的新機會。由於全球電子商務市場的興起，貿易額已經超過 12 兆歐元以上[41]，但電子商務的跨國交易對於中小企業的成本負擔高過對大型企業，但即便是小型的線上（online）企業也可以與全球的消費者進行電子商務。作為全球最大的服務出口者，歐盟應在穩健的地位中，從電子商務受益[42]。

　　數位革命亦意謂著消費者保護與在歐盟及國際消費者個人資料保護的新議題，執委會早在 2012 年即已提出個人資料保護規章法案[43]，作為資料保護穩固的法律架構，以確保完全保障歐盟人民隱私與個人資料

---

[38] European Commission, *Trade for all*, 2015 Brussels, p.10.

[39] 這 23 個締約國為澳洲、加拿大、香港、冰島、以色列、日本、韓國、列支敦斯登、紐西蘭、挪威、瑞士、中華台北、美國、歐盟、智利、哥倫比亞、哥斯大黎加、毛里西斯、墨西哥、巴拿馬、祕魯、土耳其、巴基斯坦。

[40] European Commission, *Trade for all*, 2015 Brussels, p.11.

[41] UNCTAD, Information Economy Report, 2015.

[42] European Commission, *Trade for all*, 2015 Brussels, p.12.

[43] COM (2012) 11 final.

保護的基本權力，但在貿易協定中，並未談判個人資料處理的規則[44]。

　　另一方面，數位經濟亦產生新類型的貿易障礙，特別是藉由數位管道進行的貿易，資料（包含經濟、財務、統計與學術資料）的收集、儲存、處理與傳輸、以及將資料數位化，都已經成為現代商業模式的一部分，即便是對於以製造為主的企業，也必須正視這些問題。事實上，數位化已經成為發展全球價值鏈的核心，因此資料的跨國自由流通對於歐盟的競爭力也愈來愈重要。在面臨數位經濟的挑戰下，跨國管制合作、相互承認與標準整合是最佳的方法[45]。

　　2015 年提出的數位單一市場策略（digital single market strategy）[46] 即已指明許多歐盟內部的問題，歐洲企業在全球仍面臨很多的障礙，例如不透明的規則、當地政府干預、不公平的資料本地化（data localisation）與資料儲存要求等。資料安全對於所有企業在資料處理時，是很重要的議題；數位基礎設施、加密與共同標準，對於全球價值鏈，也是重要的議題，因而也成為貿易政策的一環。在數位單一市場策略中，將進行幾個關鍵的行動，例如歐洲雲端（European Cloud）倡議、國際規模的著作權改革，因此以考慮在貿易協定中，加以規範。歐盟的目標，為建立一個全球平順的環境、無差別待遇與無不公平的資料本地化要求。因此，未來歐盟在雙邊、複邊與多邊論壇促進此一目標[47]。

　　執委會將運用自由貿易協定與服務貿易協定（TiSA），以制定電子商務與跨國資料流通的規則，並追蹤新形式的數位保護主以、完全遵循與不偏頗歐盟的資料保護與資料隱私規則，並持續在國際社會鼓吹促進與發展國際隱私與個人資料保護標準[48]。

（三）支持移動與合法的移民

歐盟各會員國的低出生率、少子化與老年化高齡社會的人口結構改變，

---

[44] European Commission, *Trade for all*, 2015 Brussels, p.12.

[45] European Commission, *Trade for all*, 2015 Brussels, p.12.

[46] COM (2015) 192 final.

[47] European Commission, *Trade for all*, 2015 Brussels, p.12.

[48] European Commission, *Trade for all*, 2015 Brussels, p.12.

勞動市場上勞動力嚴重短缺，因進移民成為補足人力短缺的重要方法。專業人士的暫時移動已經成為所有產業在國際進行商務的重要因素，專業人士與技工的移動有助於出口，可提供解決專業人力欠缺的問題。國際社會普遍限制專業人士的移動，有可能侵害貿易與投資協定的利益，同時專業人士的移動不應影響社會與勞工的法律規章[49]。

2015 年公布的歐洲移民議程（European Agenda for Migration）[50]，特別強調服務提供者暫時移動的經濟潛力，同時亦鼓吹跨領域的最佳利益合作，以期在移民與難民議題上鼓勵與第三國的合作[51]。因此，貿易政策應考慮遣返的政策架構與重新接納非法的移民[52]。

針對專業人士的移動，執委會將採取下列的措施[53]：

(1) 直接在販售特殊商品與設備（例如工程或維修服務）時，加入人員移動條款，亦納入這些商品的市場進入談判議題；

(2) 將企業內人員互流指令（Intra-corporate Transfer Directive）[54] 的利益納入貿易與投資協定，以交換貿易夥伴對歐洲專業人士的互惠待遇；

(3) 檢討藍卡指令（Blue Card Directive）[55]，以期運用專業人士進入的可能性，包含第三國國民提供暫時服務的入境與居留條件，結合歐盟在貿易協定的承諾；

(4) 在貿易協定中，促進承認專業資格；

(5) 更佳運用在貿易政策與歐盟遣返 / 重新接納、簽證便利政策間的配套措施，以期確保對歐盟有更好的結果；與

(6) 支援由歐盟提供經費的交流、培訓與其他提升能力的計畫與入口，以期在自由貿易協定有效運用人員移動條款。

---

[49] European Commission, *Trade for all*, 2015 Brussels, p.12.

[50] COM (2015) 453 final.

[51] COM (2015) 453 final.

[52] European Commission, *Trade for all*, 2015 Brussels, p.13.

[53] European Commission, *Trade for all*, 2015 Brussels, p.13.

[54] 2014 年第 66 號指令，OJ 2014 L 157/1.

[55] 2009 年第 50 號指令，OJ 2009 L 155/17-29.

（四）加強國際管制的合作

全球對於產品與服務有不同的規格要求，對於生產者往往造成額外的成本負擔，無形中形成另類的貿易保護主義，特別是對於中小企業，形成一種難以跨越的市場進入障礙。因此，加強國際管制的合作有助於促進貿易、形成全球的標準、使法規更有效率、有助於管制者更佳的運用有限的資源。因而不應限制政府的行政權，以達到正當的落實公共政策目標。歐盟與重要的貿易夥伴（例如美國與日本）在重要的國際機構，例如聯合國歐洲經濟委員會（United Nations Economic Commission for Europe）針對汽車、國際整合委員會（International Conference for Harmonisation）針對藥品、與衛生及檢疫有關國際標準制定機構（例如食品安全規約 Codex Alimentarius）針對食品，更新備忘錄；國際標準化組織，例如 ISO、IEC 與 ITU，亦扮演著重要的角色，當然 WTO 亦有助於發展好的全球治理[56]。未來，在國際管制的論壇，執委會指明管制議題，並優先維持歐洲標準；並藉由施行協定與管制合作，持續努力以消除非關稅貿易障礙[57]。

（五）確保有效率的海關管理

透過國際供應鏈，應有效率的管理商品流通，可確保貿易便捷、保護歐盟及會員國的財務與經濟利益、以及遵守貿易規範。歐盟及全球的主管機關應管理與最小化由全球貿易產生的一系列風險。因此，必須有更多的資訊交流（適當的考慮個人資料保護與營業秘密）、海關與其他機關間的協調、以及更緊密的國際合作。因此，施行 WTO 的貿易便捷規則、雙邊協定、自由貿易協定都是歐盟貿易政策明確的範圍[58]。執委會將最佳利用現行的相互行政協助與鼓勵利用由歐盟貿易夥伴許可的經濟運作綱領，以指明在全球供應鏈的風險。

---

[56] European Commission, *Trade for all*, 2015 Brussels, p.13.

[57] European Commission, *Trade for all*, 2015 Brussels, p.13.

[58] European Commission, *Trade for all*, 2015 Brussels, p.14.

（六）確保取得能源與原料

由於歐盟仰賴原料進口，因此取得能源與原料，對於歐盟的競爭力，非常重要。貿易協定可以在禁止差別待遇與過境運輸的基礎上，制定規則，例如當地成分的要求、鼓勵能源效率、貿易再生能源、依據市場原則在平順的環境確保國有企業與其他企業的競爭。因此，貿易協定可以改善取得能源與原料，這些規定必須完全尊重每一個國家對於自然資源的主權，且不應防止保護環境的行動，包括對抗氣候變遷在內。執委會並進行更廣泛的工作，以創設一個歐洲能源聯盟（European Energy Union）[59] 連結原料倡議 [60]，在每一個貿易協定規定能源與原料的專章 [61]。

（七）保護創新

創新、研究與設計，對於價值鏈的經濟非常重要，這三個領域創造歐盟三分之一的工作機會與 90% 的出口，但在其他國家未充分保護智慧財產權，而造成歐盟的創新研究與設計受到嚴重的衝擊，有時候甚至面對強制授權的威脅，特別是中小企業受到更多的影響。因此，歐盟的貿易政策應藉由保護智慧財產權的全部類型，包括專利、商標、著作權、設計、地理標示與營業秘密等，支持創新與高品質的產品。不僅應確定規則及程序，而且也應保障施行。因此，執委會將持續在自由貿易協定與 WTO 中，加強智慧財產權之保護與落實 [62]，與貿易夥伴合力打擊仿冒品，並持續促進全球衛生議程 [63] 與使貧窮國家更容易取得醫藥用品 [64]。

三、更關注中小企業的利益

進入新市場對於中小企業而言，比大企業要花費更多的成本，例如中小企業擁有較少的國際化資源、開發新市場、克服貿易與投資障礙、以及

---

[59] COM (2015) 80 final.

[60] COM (2008) 699 final.

[61] European Commission, *Trade for all*, 2015 Brussels, p.14.

[62] COM (2014) 389 final. 強調貿易、成長與智慧財產之關連性。

[63] COM (2010) 128 final.

[64] European Commission, *Trade for all*, 2015 Brussels, p.14.

遵守法規等，中小企業都面臨比大企業更大的衝擊。因此應藉由貿易協定降低對於中小企業的障礙與致力於法規整合。另一方面，中小企業不像大企業有能力建置法律諮詢部門或經濟諮詢部門，對於取得進入市場商機的資訊相對困難，因此自由貿易協定應藉由建置政府網站，以一站式（one-stop shop）提供相關產品要求的所有資訊。未來，執委會計畫 (1) 在洽簽自由貿易協定時，注意中小企業的利益，例如促進中小企業取得在外國市場產品要求的資訊、商機與可使用的支援；(2) 在貿易與投資談判上，考量中小企業的特殊性；(3) 協調會員國的貿易促進政策與中小企業國際化的努力；(4) 進行定期檢討中小企業在特別的市場所面對的障礙、與代表中小企業的機構更緊密的合作，以更佳了解中小企業的需求[65]。

四、更透明的貿易與投資政策

貿易政策愈來愈影響到歐盟與全體會員國的社會與經濟利益，因此執委會在決策時，將更考量歐洲及普世的標準與價值、核心的經濟利益、更強調永續發展、人權、租稅規避、消費者保護、負責與公平的貿易[66]。

2015 年，執委會公布一個『更好結果的更好規定』（Better regulation for better results）函示[67]，強調在貿易政策範圍的每一個明確倡議都必須進行衝擊的評估。在進行貿易協定的談判過程中，應進行永續的衝擊評估，也就是應更深入分析貿易協定可能的經濟、社會與環境衝擊，亦包含對中小企業、消費者、特別的經濟部門、人權與開發中國家的衝擊。此外，在簽署貿易協定後與貿易協定開始生效施行後，執委會也會分析這些貿易協定的經濟衝擊。

五、改革全球的投資制度

未來，歐盟將致力於改革全球投資制度，首先執委會在雙邊協定納入現代的規定，例如地主國規範權、建立公開的投資法院制度（Investment

---

[65] European Commission, *Trade for all*, 2015 Brussels, p.16.

[66] European Commission, *Trade for all*, 2015 Brussels, p.18.

[67] COM (2015) 215 final.

Court System）[68]、明確的行為規約，以避免利益衝突、由更專業的獨立法官進行審理；尋求貿易夥伴的共識，建立一個永久的國際投資法院；長遠來看，應支援在 WTO 納入投資規則；最後，應檢討 2010 年提出的國際投資政策[69]，並提出新的規劃[70]。

六、以貿易政策作為促進永續發展的手段

歐盟以貿易政策致力於永續發展，積極的作法如下[71]：

1. 普遍優惠關稅制度（Generalised Scheme of Preferences；簡稱 GSP）是一個創新的手段，以鼓勵及支援人權、永續發展與好的全球治理；

2. 綠色成長（green growth）是歐盟經濟與環境政策的一部分，環境商品與服務的開放貿易可以協助發展綠色成長。在 WTO 的 16 個會員國[72]協商環境產品協定（Environmental Goods Agreement；簡稱 EGA）[73]上，歐盟扮演一個關鍵的角色，特別是應致力於綠色科技貿易，例如再生能源的生產、垃圾管理、空氣污染的監控、對抗氣候變遷與環境保護；

3. 歐盟最近在自由貿易協定的體系上，均會包含貿易與永續發展的規定，目的就是要最大化貿易與投資的潛力，以致力於正當的工作和環境保護、對抗氣候變遷等。

七、公平與倫理的貿易制度

促進公平與倫理的貿易制度也是歐盟未來的方針，致力於發展第三國小型生產者更永續的貿易機會，尤其是在供需兩方面提高公平貿易的意

---

[68] 投資法院制度將由第一審法庭與上訴庭組成。

[69] COM (2010) 343 final.

[70] European Commission, *Trade for all*, 2015 Brussels, p.22.

[71] European Commission, *Trade for all*, 2015 Brussels, p.23.

[72] 這 16 個國家為澳洲、加拿大、中國、哥斯大黎加、中華台北、歐盟、香港、日本、韓國、紐西蘭、挪威、瑞士、新加坡、美國、以色列、土耳其與冰島。

[73] 自 2014 年 7 月以來，WTO 談判環境產品協定，環境產品協定目標為消除綠色產品的關稅、開放綠色服務市場、處理非關稅貿易障礙機制。

識。執委會將利用現行實施自由貿易協定的結構，以促進公平貿易及其他永續的制度、協助第三國小型生產者建置公平與倫理貿易制度、在歐盟境內發展提高公平貿易的倡議[74]，特別是與各會員國地方機關合作頒發『歐盟公平暨倫理貿易城市』（EU City for Fair and Ethical Trade）獎，以作為鼓勵促進公平與倫理的貿易制度。

八、振興多邊貿易制度與以雙邊貿易協定為主流

歐盟強調 WTO 多邊貿易制度是其貿易政策的基石，由於 2001 年以來杜哈回合談判延宕多年，對於很多議題無法達成共識，而使得 WTO 的多邊貿易制度受到嚴峻的挑戰。因此，有必要應盡可能恢復以 WTO 為中心的貿易談判平台，而歐盟是 WTO 架構下的一個主要談判夥伴，同時扮演著領導的角色。

　　總而言之，歐盟未來將負起鼓吹恢復 WTO 作為全球貿易自由化的發動機與最主要的貿易談判平台。WTO 應在發展與施行全球貿易規則上，扮演一個核心的角色，特別是涵蓋關稅、智慧財產、數位規範、良好的管制實踐。雖然從杜哈回合以來，WTO 談判裏足不前，許多貿易夥伴開始嘗試以雙邊與區域貿易協定，以回應延宕的全球貿易現狀。2013 年的『峇里套案』（Bali Package）已經就某些議題達成共識，而成為新的國際貿易法則。長遠來看，歐盟仍是希望回歸 WTO 作為全球貿易談判的中心，因此歐盟應促進發展 WTO 的多邊貿易規則與以雙邊貿易協定補充法律漏洞。[75]

　　但雙邊與區域貿易協定已經蓬勃發展成為規範雙邊貿易關係的主流，歐盟視自由貿易協定為全球貿易自由化的實驗室。實際上，歐盟已經與主要的貿易夥伴簽署了自由貿易協定，這些貿易夥伴為韓國、加拿大、美國、日本與中國，未來歐盟將與香港、台灣與新加坡等洽簽投資保護協定，事實上歐盟已經和遍佈全球的第三國洽簽自由貿易協定[76]，現階段雙邊自由貿易協定已經成為歐盟實現貿易政策與拓展商機的重要

---

[74] European Commission, *Trade for all*, 2015 Brussels, p.25.

[75] European Commission, *Trade for all*, 2015 Brussels, p.29.

[76] European Commission, *Trade for all*, 2015 Brussels, pp.31-33.

手段。

　　歐盟並制定簽署雙邊自由貿易協定的三個守則，即應在互惠的基礎上，有效率的開放市場與在高度的志向上規範自由貿易協定。[77] 總之，歐盟與第三國洽簽的自由貿易協定愈來愈重要，同時對於與第三國間的貿易關係及全球治理，扮演著關鍵的角色。

肆、結論

歐盟已經是全球最大且最重要的經濟與貿易實體之一，歐盟對於全球治理亦扮演著關鍵的全球角色，特別是在制定 WTO 的規則上，歐盟扮演著主導的角色。在 2008 年全球金融海嘯後，歐盟體認到貿易是促進經濟成長與創造就業的重要手段，在 WTO 的多邊架構下，歐盟致力於全球的經濟利益，由於歐盟對於共同貿易政策享有專屬的職權，因此歐盟成為主要的貿易夥伴，在國際貿易談判上，可以以一個聲音與第三國進行貿易談判，味全體會員國的利益，貫徹共同貿易政策。

　　共同貿易政策不僅包含貿易議題，而且也涵蓋投資議題，共同貿易政策包括商品與服務貿易、以及與貿易有關的智慧財產權保護議題，共同貿易政策可以說是包羅萬象。2015 年 10 月時，歐盟執委會公布了一份『貿易包羅萬象：邁向更有責任的貿易與投資政策』，揭示了歐盟貿易政策的新趨勢。

　　由歐盟的貿易政策文件可以得出結論，貿易政策是歐盟作為永續發展與核心社會模式愈來愈重要的手段，特別是在自由貿易協定納入相關的條款，以致力於永續發展、核心的勞工標準，例如廢除童工與強制勞工、工作場所的無差別待遇、結社自由與團體協約等、永續管理及保存自然資源、勞工權利及環境保護、儘速達成環境產品協定。

　　歐盟肯定多邊的貿易體制，特別是 WTO 的規則是全球貿易秩序的基礎，也應持續作為歐盟貿易政策的基石。目前 WTO 已經有多達 161 個會員國，歐盟一直是 WTO 各項貿易談判的重要角色，未來仍將在 WTO 的架構作為促進全球貿易自由化的推動者。

---

[77] European Commission, *Trade for all*, 2015 Brussels, p.30.

　　總而言之，歐盟的貿易政策以涵蓋人權、社會、環境等不同的面向，尤其是永續發展已經是一個核心概念。也就是歐盟的貿易政策已經轉為永續發展及創造更多就業的手段，這也反應在不同的面向，例如政府採購市場 [78]、創造就業及優惠中小企業的產業政策、環境保護、對抗氣候變遷、與加強歐盟在全球治理的主導角色。

---

[78] 政府採購市場是一個適當的經濟政策工具，可以達到生態永續發展短期、中期與長期的目標，並能促進全球更高的社會標準。

The New Trend of EU Trade Policy

Prof. Dr. Li-Jiuan Chen-Rabich, LL.M

Professor of Graduate Institute of European Studies, Tamkang University

Jean Monnet Chair on European Trade Law

Abstract

The EU has become one of the largest and most important trade and economic unit in the international community. The EU plays a key global actor for the establishment of the global governance, in particular rules of the WTO. After the global financial crisis in 2008, the EU has recognized that trade is an important tool for the economic growth and jobs creation. The EU contributes to the global economic interests within the multilateral framework of the WTO. The EU is a main trade partner due to its exclusive right for the common trade policy. As a consequence, the EU can speak with one voice in the international trade negotiation and take charge of the common trade policy on behalf of member states' interest.

The common trade policy is very comprehensive. The EU has published a document "Trade for all: Towards a more responsible trade and investment policy" in October 2015. Trade policy is a more and more important tool for the EU's sustainable development and core social model. Trade is a driver of economic prosperity and sustainable development.

The EU affirms multilateral trade system and especially recognizes trade rules of the WTO as basis of global trade order. These trade rules of the WTO are also the fundament of the EU trade policy. Currently, the WTO has more 161 members. The EU is always one of the important trade negotiators within the WTO framework. The EU will play its key role to promote the liberalization of global trade and global economic governance.

The EU's trade policy is very comprehensive and includes social, economic, environmental issues and respect for human rights. The sustainable development has become a core concept of the EU's trade policy. The trade policy has transformed into a tool for sustainable development, jobs creation and other aspects such as public procurement market, jobs creation and privileged industrial policy for small- and medium-sized enterprises, environmental protection, measures against climate change and strengthening the EU's leading role in the global governance.

This article works on the new trend of the EU trade policy. First of all, it describes the EU's position as a global actor with its integration in the international community. In particular, the EU plays a leading role within the WTO. Trade is an important driver for the economic growth and creation of jobs after the global financial crisis. Therefore, it concludes the new trend of the EU trade policy.

I. Introduction

The European Union (EU) has become one of the largest trade and economic units in the world. The euro has been introduced as a single legal currency since 2002 in the euro area. The euro is the second important reserve currency in the international financial market. After the global financial crisis since 2008, the EU has recognized that trade is an important tool to drive the economic growth and creation of jobs. Hence, the EU has contributed to economic benefits with the globalization. The EU wishes to strengthen the trade relation with the third countries under the World Trade Organization (WTO) trade framework.

This article works on the new trend of the EU trade policy. First of all, it describes the EU's position as a global actor with its integration in the international community. In particular, the EU plays a leading role within the WTO. Trade is an important driver for the economic growth and creation of jobs after the global financial crisis. Therefore, it concludes the new trend of the EU trade policy.

II. The current position of the EU in the international community

The European Union is a result of the regional integration after the World War II. With the trend, the EU has developed into a unique trade and economic unit in the international community. The EU has also become a model for the regional economic integration in the world. The EU has been established on the basis of legal framework of the fundamental treaties and developed from the customs union, the single market to the economic and monetary union. The economic and monetary union plays a new milestone for the European integration.

Currently, the EU has 28 member states.[1] The EU has combined all member states' economic power. Therefore, the EU has become a political unit as an active global actor in the international community. Nowadays, the EU has over 500 million people. The Euro has been a single currency since 2002 in the Euro Area with 19 member states.[2] The Euro Area has established a solid economic unit whose economic power can't be ignored.

---

[1] They are Germany, France, Italy, Netherlands, Luxemburg, Belgium, United Kingdom, Denmark, Ireland, Greece, Spain, Portugal, Austria, Finland, Sweden, Estonia, Latvia, Lithuania, the Czech Republic, Slovakia, Hungry, Poland, Slovenia, Malta, Cyprus, Bulgaria, Romania and Croatia.

[2] They are Germany, France, Italy, Netherlands, Luxemburg, Belgium, Ireland, Greece, Spain, Portugal, Austria, Finland, Estonia, Latvia, Lithuania, Slovakia, Slovenia, Malta, Cyprus.

To sum up, the global financial crisis and the subsequent European sovereign debt crisis has resulted that the EU has developed a new economic governance model. The "Europe 2020 Strategy"[3] was introduced in June 2020 and has replaced the "Lisbon Strategy".[4] The "Europe 2020 Strategy" has outlined the new policy until 2020 to aim at smart, sustainable and inclusive growth.

The WTO established in 1995 has become the most important international economic organization. Both the EU and its member states are formal members since the establishment of the WTO. The rules of the WTO are legal binding to the EU and its member states. The European Commission is representative due to the common trade policy on behalf of the EU's interests with one voice within the WTO. As a result, the EU has become the main negotiation partner to other WTO members.

With the trend of globalization and liberalization of international economic rules within the WTO framework, the EU has further expanded the trade policy to other fields of economic activities. After the complete of the Single Market in the end of 1992, the EU has followed this development and has established a common external economic policy beyond the goods trade. The Lisbon Treaty in 2009 has reformed the common trade policy under the WTO framework. As a consequence, the EU has exclusive power to execute common trade policy. The EU is the only one actor with one voice to participate in the decision-making of the WTO. To sum up, the Lisbon Treaty has strengthened the global actor of the EU. The EU has more actively taken part in the global economic governance.

The advanced developed countries, the emerging countries, the developing countries and the less developed countries have different opinions and concerns related to the global economic issues since the

---

[3] COM (2010) 2020 final.

[4] COM (2001) 641 final.

Doha Round in 2001. Finally, the Bali Package as new international economic rules has agreed within the WTO in December 2013. The multilateral trade framework of the WTO has confronted challenges with the lengthy Doha Round. Therefore, the regional trade agreement and bilateral free trade agreement have step by step replaced the WTO rules. The regional trade agreement and bilateral free trade agreement have also become important mechanism for the global governance. The EU and the USA have regular transatlantic economic dialogue and have active negotiation about the Agreement on Transatlantic Trade and Investment Partnership (TTIP). The EU has also maintained a good dialogue mechanism with China. The USA, the EU and China have built a new triangle trade relation and a new balance of economic powers. The goal of the European trade policy is to help European enterprises to explore new business opportunities and export markets.

The trade policy plays a key element of the "Europe 2020 Strategy". Trade is also a driver of economic prosperity.[5] The EU has used trade as an important tool to complete "Europe 2020 Strategy". Meanwhile, the EU has increasingly weighed the investment issues. Trade and investment depend and complement each other. Investment has also become a part of the common trade policy. The investment policy also contributes to the goal of the "Europe 2020 Strategy". Obviously, investment has become one of important tools of the European global governance. The free trade agreement of the EU has increasingly included the provision of investment protection. The EU has gradually taken bilateral free trade agreement with third countries to carry out its rules of investment protection. As a result, trade and investment have close combination. The EU's free trade agreement of new generation has further included rules of investment protection. After the deep and wide economic integration,

---

[5] European Commission staff working document, *Trade as a driver of prosperity*, SEC (2010) 1269.

the EU has become a new "Economic Superpower" in the international community.

III. New trend of EU trade policy

1. Background

The global financial crisis resulted in the economic recession in the EU. Hence, the first priority of the European Commission is promoting employment, growth and investment. Trade is not only a driver for economic growth, but also a part of national structural reform and EU investment plan.[6] Trade and investment are two tools to achieve objectives. Meanwhile, enterprises, labors and consumers in the EU can benefit from trade.

The EU is the largest importer and exporter of goods and services in the world. The EU is not only the largest foreign investor, but also the most important destination of foreign direct investment. To sum up, the EU is a key trade partner in the world. Both EU citizens and citizens of third countries have benefits from trade.[7]

The European Commission published a document "Trade for all" in October 2015. This document has outlined the new trend of the EU trade policy. The trade policy plays a more and more important role in the future, in particular to take the responsibility for promoting protection for consumer and labor, economic effects of small- and medium-sized enterprises. The trade policy must be more effective and transparent. The trade policy has to reflect both benefits and values.

The document includes:

(1) Trade and investment as a powerful driver for economic growth and

---

[6] COM (2014) 903 final.

[7] European Commission, *Trade for all*, 2015 Brussels, p.7.

jobs creation;

(2) Effective execution of policies for the current economic situation and concrete objectives;

(3) More transparent trade and investment policy;

(4) Trade and investment policy on the basis of the EU values;

(5) Contribution of the planed negotiations to establishing global governance.

2. *Trade and investment as powerful engines of economic growth and jobs creation*

Trade was not important for the EU economy. After the global financial crisis and economic recession, the EU has realized that trade is an important tool for economic recovery in the future. Trade can bring the EU many benefits, such as jobs, economic growth, business opportunities and so on.[8] Export opportunities also support small- and medium-sized enterprises to explore markets of third countries. Larger companies export more goods and services outside of the EU. Export will be the fastest way for economic growth and jobs creation.

Trade is a two-way process. Import is also important for the EU economy. Opening up the EU market to third countries is a main tool for promoting trade and enhancing productivity and private investment. The development of global value chain stresses the interdependence between import and export, which plays an important role for the functioning of the economy and international competitiveness of EU companies.

Investment is another important element to the economic recovery and growth. Internal and external investment is essential to infrastructure. Investment can link the European economy with the global value chain. The EU's "Investment plan for Europe" contributes to enhancing investment and making smarter use of new and existing

---

[8] European Commission, *Trade for all*, 2015 Brussels, p.8.

financial resources. The EU's policy on foreign direct investment has to support objectives and priorities of the "Europe 2020 Strategy".[9]

To strengthen the EU's capacity to benefit from trade and investment, the European Commission has actively developed bilateral free trade agreement in order to complement the EU's engagement at the WTO. The EU has concluded or is negotiating bilateral free trade agreements with its trade partners all over the world. The bilateral free trade agreements cover more than a third of EU trade. It could reach two thirds if all ongoing negotiations are concluded. As a consequence, bilateral free trade agreement is more and more important to establish international economic rules.

> *The EU has underlined that trade policy has to strengthen the EU's position in the global value chain and to support economic activities such as manufacturing of components and final products, services, research, design and marketing, assembly, distribution and maintenance.* [10]

With the trend of globalization, EU trade policy has already expanded from traditional tariff to vital issues such as public procurement, competition, subsidies, sanitary and phytosanitary barriers. It is essential to ensure a level playing field in market access. Free trade agreement can partly contribute to this objective. The bilateral free trade agreement of new generation includes some provisions related to non-tariff issues such as public procurement, environmental protection, protection of investment. To sum up, the bilateral free trade agreement has increasingly become important tool to implement the EU trade policy, for example Free Trade Agreement between the EU and South Korea, Comprehensive Economic and Trade Agreement between the EU and Canada, ongoing negotiation of TTIP between the EU and the USA.

---

[9] COM (2014) 130 final.

[10] European Commission, *Trade for all*, 2015 Brussels, p.10.

On the other side, trade policy can support domestic structural reform, more investment in infrastructure, skills and research, less red tape, better access to financial resources and development in order to enhance the EU's capacity to take advantage of open markets. All of them are essential to ensure the EU's position in the global supply chain. Trade agreements support contributions to international standards of transparency and good governance, in particular promoting trade in services, facilitating digital trade, supporting mobility and addressing migration, reinforcing international regulatory cooperation in bilateral negotiations, regional and global solutions, ensuring the efficient management of customs, securing access to energy and raw materials, protecting innovation and intellectual property rights like patent, trademark, copyright, design, geographical indications and trade secrets.

3. Focusing on the advantages of small- and medium-sized enterprises

The small- and medium-sized enterprises are backbone of the EU economy. In comparison to larger companies, the small- and medium-sized enterprises have fewer resources for internationalization, accessing new markets, overcoming trade and investment barriers and complying with regulation. The small- and medium-sized enterprises have to face more difficult market requirements and business barriers. Therefore, the European Commission has taken into account specifications of small- and medium-sized enterprises in all chapters of trade and investment negotiations, including dedicated web portals to facilitate access to information on product requirements in foreign markets, opportunities provided by the free trade agreements and available support. On the other hand, the European Commission has coordinated with national trade promotion policies and set up government websites acting as a one-stop shop for all information on relevant product requirements. Regular surveys on barriers small- and medium-sized enterprises face in specific markets have been established. The European Commission has also cooperated more closely with representative bodies of small- and medium-sized enterprises to better figure out their needs.[11]

4. A more transparent trade and investment policy

Trade policy is a more and more issue of concern in the international economic community, in particular in the negotiations of the bilateral free trade agreements. Trade policy has step by step influenced on the EU's social and regulatory model such as environmental conditions, product requirements, investment protection, consumer information, labor interests and the respect of human rights. As a consequence, the European Commission has to take into account these issues seriously and have a transparent and open policymaking process to react on people's concerns with regard to the EU's social model. The European Commission must promote European and universal standards and values alongside key economic interests, put a greater emphasis on sustainable development, human rights, tax evasion, consumer protection and responsible and fair trade.[12]

The EU's investment policy has also to respond to the public's expectations and concerns by reinforcing corporate social responsibility and due diligence across the production chain with a focus on the respect of human rights and social and environmental aspects of value chain. Meanwhile, member state governments must also carry out their responsibility to enforce EU regulations on goods and services on imported as well as domestically produced products.

According to the Communication "Better regulation for better results"[13], the European Commission carries out sustainability impact

---

[11] European Commission, *Trade for all*, 2015 Brussels, p.18.

[12] European Commission, *Trade for all*, 2015 Brussels, p.7.

[13] COM (2015) 215 final.

assessment during the negotiation of major trade agreements. The sustainability impact assessment has a more in-depth analysis of the potential economic, social and environmental impacts of trade agreements, including on small- and medium-sized enterprises, consumers, specific economic sectors, on human rights and on developing countries. The European Commission also analyses the economic impacts of free trade agreements after their conclusion and carries out ex post evaluation after their implementation. Sustainability impact assessments and evaluations are very important for formulating sound, transparent and evidence-based trade policies.[14] Trade and investment is an important instrument to promote sustainable development, respect human rights, high labor and environmental standards, health and safety protection all over the world. Hence, trade and investment policy must work closely with other instruments of EU external action.[15]

5. *Reform of the global investment system*

The issue of investment protection has recently become a hot topic. The need for reform is now acknowledged all over the world. The EU will contribute to the reform of the global investment regime in the near future. The EU has competence for investment protection since the Lisbon Treaty in December 2009. The EU has made reform the investment system as a priority, for example in the context of the TTIP.[16]

First of all, the EU has provided the rules of investment protection such as right of the state to regulate and arbitration in the bilateral free trade agreements with third countries. The EU puts stronger emphasis on the reform of the investor-state dispute settlement that is composed of a Tribunal of First Instance and an Appeal Tribunal. It is necessary to

---

[14] European Commission, *Trade for all*, 2015 Brussels, p.18.

[15] European Commission, *Trade for all*, 2015 Brussels, p.18.

[16] http://trade.ec.europa.eu/doclib/docs/2015/september/tradoc_153807.pdf.

have a clear code of conduct to avoid conflicts of interest, independent judges with high technical and legal qualifications. The EU is actively engaged with partners to build consensus for a fully-fledged, permanent International Investment Court. In the long run, the EU will contribute to the incorporation of investment rules into the WTO, in order to set up a clearer, more legitimate and more comprehensive system. The EU will also review its former investment policy and set up a new investment policy in order to boost investment activities.[17]

6. *Trade as a tool to promote sustainable development*

The EU considers trade policy as a component of the EU's 2020 Strategy that puts emphasis on sustainable and inclusive growth. Trade openness is an important instrument to lift developing countries out of poverty. The developing countries can reap the benefits of globalization.[18] The EU's General System of Preference (GSP) for exports from developing countries has contributed to promoting the development of developing countries and integrating them into the global value chain, including the development of poorer countries, high social and environmental standards, respect for human rights, and good global governance.[19]

The EU has also used trade policy to promote the social and environmental pillars of sustainable development. The EU plays a leading role in international negotiations for an environmental goods agreement with 16 other major WTO members.[20] Green growth is a part of the EU's economic and environmental policies. Opening up trade in environmental goods and services can help develop green growth. The

---

[17] European Commission, *Trade for all*, 2015 Brussels, pp.21-22.

[18] SEC (2010) 1269, p.4.

[19] European Commission, *Trade for all*, 2015 Brussels, p.22.

[20] They are Australia, Canada, China, Costa Rica, Chinese Taipei, the European Union, Hong Kong, Japan, Korea, New Zealand, Norway, Switzerland, Singapore, United States, Israel, Turkey and Iceland.

EU is actively working on liberalizing trade in environmental goods and services at multilateral level in the WTO, and in its free trade agreements, in particular in the fields of trade in vital green technologies such as renewable energy generation, waste management and air pollution control. The EU also contributes to combatting climate change and protecting the environment. Recently, the EU has regulated systematically provisions on trade and sustainable development in free trade agreements with third countries. The objectives are to maximize the potential of increased trade and investment to decent work and to environmental protection, including the fight against climate change. The EU also engages with partner countries in a cooperation fostering transparency and civil society involvement. The EU has taken into account sustainable development considerations in all relevant areas of free trade agreements, for example energy and raw materials, public procurement, labor rights, environmental protection, occupational health and safety, decent working conditions and the fight against climate change.[21]

7. *Fair and ethical trade system*

Nowadays, there is no channel of information about access to fair and ethical trade system for both producers and EU consumers. The EU will use the existing structure for implementation of free trade agreements to promote fair trade and other sustainability assurance schemes. The EU puts emphasis on fair and ethical trade more systematically in the upcoming of the EU "Aid for trade" strategy and report on fair trade-related projects. The EU contributes to fair and ethical trade schemes to small producers in third countries. The EU will support to work in international for a, such as the International Trade Center, to gather market data in relation to fair and ethical trade markets. In the long term, the EU will develop awareness-raising activities in the EU, in particular

---

[21] European Commission, *Trade for all*, 2015 Brussels, p.23.

working with local authorities in all member states via the possible launch of an "EU City for Fair and Ethical Trade" award.[22]

8. *Reinvigorating the multilateral trading system, but new trend with bilateral trade agreement*

The EU emphasizes the multilateral trade system of the WTO as the cornerstone of EU trade policy. Due to the failure to conclude the Doha Round negotiation since 2001, it is necessary to do everything possible to recover the centrality of the WTO as a trade negotiation forum. The EU is one of the key negotiators and plays a leading role under the WTO framework.

As a consequence, the EU will take charge of advocating reestablishment of the WTO as the driver of global trade liberalization and the preeminent forum for trade negotiations. The WTO has to play a central role in developing and enforcing the rules of global trade, from intellectual property to customs, from digital to good regulatory practice. Although the WTO has made less progress since the Doha Round negotiation, many trading partners have tried to develop bilateral and regional agreement to response to changing the hesitant global trade realities. The 2013 Bali Package has completed some issues and set up new international trade rules. However, bilateral and regional trade agreements have been further developed. The EU considers free trade agreements as a laboratory for global liberalization. In the long run, the EU wants to return the WTO to the center of global trade negotiating activity. The EU has to develop future WTO proposals to fill the gaps in the multilateral rulebook and reduce fragmentation from solutions achieved in bilateral negotiations.[23]

The EU has also developed its bilateral free trade agreements with

---

[22] European Commission, *Trade for all*, 2015 Brussels, p.25.

[23] European Commission, *Trade for all*, 2015 Brussels, p.29.

major trade partners such as South Korea, Canada, the United States, Japan and China. The EU will explore launching negotiations on investment with Hong Kong, Taiwan and Singapore. Actually, the EU has developed bilateral free trade agreements with third countries all over the world.[24] The bilateral free trade agreement is in fact an important tool to achieve the EU trade policy and explore business opportunities.

The EU has established three guiding principles for bilateral free trade agreements, namely free trade agreements must regulate reciprocal and effective opening, based on a high level of ambition.[25] To sum up, the bilateral free trade agreements between the EU and third countries are more and more important than before and play a essential role for the trade relations with third countries and global governance.

IV. Conclusion

The EU has become one of the largest and most important trade and economic unit in the international community. The EU plays a key global actor for the establishment of the global governance, in particular rules of the WTO. After the global financial crisis in 2008, the EU has recognized that trade is an important tool for the economic growth and jobs creation. The EU contributes to the global economic interests within the multilateral framework of the WTO. The EU is a main trade partner due to its exclusive right for the common trade policy. As a consequence, the EU can speak with one voice in the international trade negotiation and take charge of the common trade policy on behalf of member states' interest.

The common trade policy includes not only trade issues, but also investment issues. The common trade policy covers trade of goods and

---

[24] European Commission, *Trade for all*, 2015 Brussels, pp.31-33.

[25] European Commission, *Trade for all*, 2015 Brussels, p.30.

services. The issue of trade related to the intellectual property rights is also inclusive within the common trade policy. To sum up, the common trade policy is very comprehensive. The EU has published a document "Trade for all: Towards a more responsible trade and investment policy" in October 2015.

Trade policy is a more and more important tool for the EU's sustainable development and core social model, in particular in provisions of the bilateral free trade agreement between the EU and third countries. Namely, trade policy is a tool to achieve protection of labor interests such as abolishing child labor and forced labor, non-discrimination at the workplace, freedom of association, collective tariff, sustainable management and maintenance of natural resources, environmental protection and environmental product agreement. Trade is a driver of economic prosperity and sustainable development.

The EU affirms multilateral trade system and especially recognizes trade rules of the WTO as basis of global trade order. These trade rules of the WTO are also the fundament of the EU trade policy. Currently, the WTO has more 161 members. The EU is always one of the important trade negotiators within the WTO framework. The EU will play its key role to promote the liberalization of global trade and global economic governance.

As a consequence, the EU's trade policy is very comprehensive and includes social, economic, environmental issues and respect for human rights. The sustainable development has become a core concept of the EU's trade policy. The trade policy has transformed into a tool for sustainable development, jobs creation and other aspects such as public procurement market, jobs creation and privileged industrial policy for small- and medium-sized enterprises, environmental protection, measures against climate change and strengthening the EU's leading role in the global governance.

Legal View of the Free Trade Agreements between the EU and Asian Countries

Prof. Dr. Yumiko Nakanishi

Professor of Graduate School of Law, Hitotsubashi University, Tokyo

I. Introduction

The EU (European Union) and some Asian countries concluded or are negotiating Free Trade Agreements (FTAs). Recent FTAs are no longer simple 'trade' agreements but are comprehensive documents that include not only goods but also services, investments and intellectual property rights. Simultaneously, the EU has been urging for concluding binding political agreements.

Firstly, the structure of the EU's external competence and external actions will be explained. Secondly, an overview of FTAs between the EU and Asian countries will be examined. Thirdly, some issues like geographical indication (GI), investment, environmental issues and human rights will be discussed. Fourthly, FTAs will be considered with political principles. Finally, this paper will be concluded in the global context, considering the World Trade Organization (WTO), Transatlantic Trade and Investment Partnership (TTIP), Trans-Pacific Partnership (TPP) and other FTAs.

II. Structure of the EU's external competences and external actions

1. *The EU*

The EU has a legal personality (Article 47 TEU) and competences to conclude agreements with third countries or international organisations (Article 216 TFEU). It means that not only the Member States but also the EU can conclude agreements. In some cases only the EU can conclude agreements, not the Member States.

2. *The Treaty of Lisbon*

The Treaty of Lisbon entered into force on 1 December 2009. The Treaty amended the EC Treaty (the Treaty establishing the European Community, TEC) and the EU Treaty (the Treaty on the European Union, TEU). The TEC became the Treaty on functioning of the EU (TFEU). Moreover, the Lisbon Treaty changed the existing TEC and TEU to a great extent in the field of external actions.

According to the Treaty of Lisbon, first, the TEU has a special title, i.e. title V 'general provisions on the EU's external action and specific provisions on the common foreign and security policy' in Articles 21-46, and the TFEU also has a distinct part, i.e. part five 'the Union's external cation' in Articles 205-219. Before the Treaty of Lisbon, external issues were sporadically laid down in the TEC and TEU; however, after the Treaty, external action has a distinct title or part in each Treaty. Second, after the Treaty of Lisbon, the EU competences are systematically stipulated. Third, the implied external competences that the EU's court has developed are detailed explicitly in the TFEU.

3. *EU's external competences*

(1) The principle of the conferral

The EU is not a State. Therefore, the Member States confer competences on the EU and subsequently the EU can actively attain the objectives in the TEU and TFEU. It means that if the Member States do not confer competences on the EU, it cannot take any measures. It is the principle of the conferral (Article 5 TEU).

(2) The category of competences

The competences that the Member States confer on the EU are different. The categories of competences are as follows: exclusive competences, shared competences, competences to carry out actions to support, coordinate or supplement the actions of the Member States and special competences for the common foreign and security policy (Article 2 TFEU). In the field of exclusive competences, only the EU may legislate and adopt measures and conclude treaties. For example, the EU has exclusive competence in the fields of customs union, common commercial policy and monetary policy (Article 3 TFEU). In this case, the EU can conclude a bilateral agreement with a third country, and the Member States cannot negotiate nor conclude an agreement with a third country. On the other hand, in the field of shared competences, both the EU and Member States may legislate and adopt measures and conclude treaties. For example, the EU has shared competence in the field of environmental policy, consumer protection and transport (Article 4 TFEU). In that case, principally, the EU concludes agreements with the Member States and a third country. The agreements will be the alleged mixed agreements. In the field of culture and education, the EU has very weak competence, which is competence to carry out actions to support, coordinate or supplement the actions of the Member States (Article 6 TFEU). Which competence the EU has depends on its activity field.

(3) Free Trade Agreements and EU competences

   (i) GATT and WTO

The EU was not a member of GATT (General Agreement on Tariff and Trade); however, it is a member of the World Trade Organization (WTO). GATT was signed on 30 October 1947. At that time, the European Economic Community (EEC) did not exist. Moreover, the EEC could not become a member of GATT because only states could be its members. Furthermore, the WTO was established on 1 January 1995. At that time, the EEC had a legal personality and competence in the field of trade. The international presence of the EEC in that field was already remarkable. The WTO agreement referred to the EEC explicitly (Article XI Marrakesh Agreement establishing the World Trade Organization). Therefore, the EEC (now, the EU) could become a member. In the Commission's opinion, the EEC could conclude the WTO agreement on its own accord. However, in Opinion 1/94 of the EU's Court, the EEC would have exclusive competence for the GATT 1995 but would have shared competence with the Member States for General Agreement on Trade in Services (GATS) and Agreement on Trade-Related Aspects of Intellectual Property Rights (TRIPs). As a result, the EEC (now, the EU) concluded the WTO agreement with the Member States together in the form of a mixed agreement.

  (ii) FTA and EU competences

The EU has exclusive competences in the field of common commercial policy (Article 3 (1) (e) TFEU). According to the amendment specified by the Treaty of Lisbon, common commercial policy contains not only trade in goods and tariff but also trade in services, the commercial aspects of intellectual property and foreign direct investment (Article 207 TFEU).

With respect to traditional FTAs, i.e. if FTAs mainly enumerate trade or trade related issues, the EU might have exclusive competences for the agreements. As a result, the EU could conclude FTAs on its own accord, without participation of the Member States. However, if an agreement is a comprehensive agreement and contains various elements, the FTA would enumerate other fields of competence that do not belong to the common commercial policy. If the subjects of the FTAs belong to shared competence fields, the EU will have to conclude those FTAs with the Member States.

For example, South Korea concluded a comprehensive FTA with the EU. As a result, not only the EU but also its Member States concluded the FTA together. The legal basis of concluding the FTA is not only Article 207 TFEU but also Articles 91 (transport), 100 (2) (transport) and 167 (3) (culture) TFEU[1]. The EU and Singapore finished the negotiations for a comprehensive FTA on 17 October 2014. It has not yet been formally adopted because it is uncertain whether the provisional agreement will be concluded by the EU unaided or with the participation of its Member States. The European Commission asked the EU's Court according to Article 218 paragraph 11 whether the EU would have exclusive or shared competences for the related FTA[2]. The Court has not yet expressed its opinion.

III. Current situation of the FTAs between the EU and Asian countries

The EU and Asian countries have concluded or are negotiating Free Trade

---

[1] OJ of the EU 2011 L127/1, Council Decision of 16 September 2010.

[2] Opinion 2/15, OJ of the EU 2015 C 363/18.

Agreements (FTAs).

1. *South Korea*

South Korea is the first country that concluded an FTA with the EU. The Council of the EU authorised the Commission to negotiate an FTA with South Korea on 23 April 2007. Two and a half years later, the agreement was initialled on 15 October 2009. The FTA entered into force on 1 July 2011. It is composed of 15 chapters: chapter 1 'objectives and general definitions', chapter 2 'national treatment and market access for goods', chapter 3 'trade remedies', chapter 4 'technical barriers to trade', chapter 5 'sanitary and phytosanitary measures', chapter 6 'customs and trade facilitation', chapter 7 'trade in services, establishment and electronic commerce', chapter 8 'payment and capital movements', chapter 9 'government procurement', chapter 10 'intellectual property', chapter 11 'competition', chapter 12 'transparency', chapter 13 'trade and sustainable development', chapter 14 'dispute settlement' and chapter 15 'institutional, general and final provisions'.

The negotiations for the FTA between the EU and South Korea began, and the agreement was initialled before the Treaty of Lisbon; however, the FTA entered into force after the Treaty of Lisbon. Thus, it is considered as an FTA of the new generation. At the same time, this FTA is differentiated from other very recent FTAs due to its competence of the EU.

2. *ASEAN*

The Association of South East Asian Nations (ASEAN) was established on 8 August 1967 in Bangkok, Thailand, by the ASEAN Declaration. Originally, it had the following five members: Indonesia, Malaysia, Philippines, Singapore and Thailand. Subsequently, Brunei (1984), Vietnam (1995), Myanmar and Laos (1997) and Cambodia (1999) became members. ASEAN is composed of all ten Southeast Asian countries. ASEAN is based on moderate mutual cooperation; moreover, decision-making is done through consultation or consensus.

The EU began to negotiate for a region-to-region FTA with ASEAN in 2007 but paused in 2009 and started negotiating with each ASEAN country individually. In contrast, Japan began to negotiate for a comprehensive economic partnership agreement (AJCEP) with the Member States of ASEAN on 13 April 2005. It should take a note that Japan did not conclude the agreement with ASEAN itself, but the Member States of the ASEAN[3]. ASEAN differs from the EU and it is unclear that ASEAN has a legal personality and legal capacity independently from the Member States of ASEAN[4], although ASEAN charter lays down that ASEAN has a legal personality (Article 3)[5]. ASEAN is AJCEP was signed on 14 April 2008 and entered into force in December 2008 (Indonesia is excepted). Japan also concluded an FTA with Singapore (November 2002), Malaysia (July 2006), Thailand (November 2007), Indonesia (July 2008), Brunei (July 2008), Philippines (December 2008) and Vietnam (October 2009).

(1) Singapore

Negotiations for a comprehensive free trade agreement between the EU and Singapore were launched in 2007 and concluded on 17 October 2014. The initialled agreement should be approved by the Commission, agreed by the Council and consented by the European Parliament. As stated before, on 10 July 2015, the Commission asked the EU's Court whether the EU independently would have

---

[3]   http://www.mofa.go.jp/policy/economy/fta/asean/agreement.pdf; Article 1 (h) lays down, '"parties" means Japan and those ASEAN Member States for which this Agreement has entered into force collectively'.

[4]   Cf. Marise Cremona, David Kleimann, Joris Larik, Rena Lee and Pascal Vennesson, *ASEAN's External Agreements*, Cambridge University Press, 2015, pp. 26-27.

[5]   Article 3 lays down, 'ASEAN, as an inter-governmental organization, is hereby conferred legal personality'.

competence to sign and conclude the FTA with Singapore, more specifically, which provisions of the agreement would fall within the EU's exclusive competence, which would fall within the EU's shared competence and if there would be any provision that would fall within the exclusive competence of the Member States[6]. The case Opinion 2/15 is pending before the EU's Court.

The initialled agreement is composed of the following 17 chapters: preamble and chapter 1 'objectives and general definitions', chapter 2 'national treatment and market access for goods', chapter 3 'trade remedies', chapter 4 'technical barriers to trade', chapter 5 'sanitary and phytosanitary measures', chapter 6 'customs and trade facilitation', chapter 7 'non-tariff barriers to trade and investment in renewable energy generation', chapter 8 'services, establishment and electronic commerce', chapter 9 'investment protection', chapter 10 'government procurement', chapter 11 'intellectual property', chapter 12 'competition and related matters', chapter 13 'trade and sustainable development', chapter 14 'transparency', chapter 15 'dispute settlement', chapter 16 'mediation mechanism' and chapter 17 'institutional, general and final provisions'.

(2) Vietnam

The negotiations for an FTA between the EU and Vietnam were launched in June 2012, and the FTA became final on 2 December 2015. It is composed of the following 18 chapters: Preamble and chapter 1 'objectives and general definitions', chapter 2 'national treatment and market access for goods', chapter 3 'trade remedies', chapter 4 'protocol concerning the definition of the concept of "originating products" and methods of administrative cooperation', chapter 5 'customs and trade facilitation', chapter 6 'technical barriers to trade', chapter 7 'sanitary and phytosanitary measures',

---

[6] Opinion 2/15, OJ of the EU 2015 C 363/18.

chapter 8 'trade in services, investment and e-commerce', chapter 9 'government procurement', chapter 10 'state owned enterprises, enterprises granted special rights or privileges and monopolies', chapter 11 'competition policy', chapter 12 'intellectual policy', chapter 13 'dispute settlement', chapter 14 'non-tariff barriers to trade and investment in renewable energy generation', chapter 15 'trade and sustainable development', chapter 16 'cooperation and capacity building', chapter 17 'institutional, general and final provisions' and chapter 18 'transparency'.

(3)   Other ASEAN countries

The EU and Malaysia began to negotiate an FTA officially on 5 October 2010, which is ongoing. The EU launched negotiations for an FTA with Thailand on 6 March 2013. The EU has not yet started negotiating FTAs with Indonesia, Cambodia, Philippines, Brunei, Myanmar and Laos. However, due to the comprehensive political reform and advances in democracy, the EU did lift the economic sanctions it had imposed on Myanmar.

3. *Japan*

Negotiations regarding the free trade agreement between Japan and the EU date back to 28 May 2011, just after the Fukushima accident[7]. Both sides agreed to start a scoping process to conclude an FTA. During that period, the EU and South Korea concluded an FTA that entered into force in July 2011, as mentioned above. Facing such a change, Japanese economic circles began demanding a similar agreement with the EU because Korean and Japanese products compete to some extent. Following the successful conclusion of the scoping exercise, the

---

[7]   Yumiko Nakanishi, 'Economic Partnership Agreement between Japan and the European Union and Legal Issues: A focus on investment', Hitotsubashi Journal of law and politics, vol. 44, p. 19, http://hermes-ir.lib.hit-u.ac.jp/rs/bitstream/10086/27744/1/HJlaw0440000190.pdf.

European Commission decided to ask the EU Council for a negotiating mandate for the Japan–EU negotiations in July 2012. The first round of negotiations was conducted in Brussels from 15 to 19 April 2013. The deadline for the negotiations from the EU side was set for one year. One year later, the EU reviewed the negotiations process and decided to continue negotiating with Japan. Most recently, the sixteenth round of negotiations regarding trade in goods, services, intellectual property rights, non-tariff measures, governmental procurement and investment on the Japan–EU Economic Partnership Agreement (EPA) took place from 11 April to 15 April 2016.

4. China

The EU launched negotiations not for an FTA but a comprehensive investment agreement, which are ongoing.

IV. Character of the FTAs between the EU and Asian countries

Recent FTAs are no more simple 'trade' agreements and are becoming comprehensive. They include trade not only in goods but also in services, investment, intellectual property rights and sustainable development.

1. Investment

(1) Case of South Korea

The connection between trade and investment is emphasized in the FTA between the EU and South Korea. For example, the preamble uses the phrases 'liberalising and expanding mutual trade and investment', 'governing their trade and investment' and 'reduce or eliminate the barriers to mutual trade and investment'. 'Trade and investment' is similar to a set. Article 1.1 (b) states that one of the objectives of the Agreement is to liberalise trade in services and investment and Article 1.1 (h) of the FTA states that one of the objectives of the Agreement is to promote foreign investment. However, the FTA does not have a chapter for investment and does not rule Investor-State dispute settlement (ISDS). This is because the EU and South Korea began to negotiate an FTA in 2007 and concluded this on 15 October 2009 before the Treaty of Lisbon. It means that the EU did not have exclusive competence in the field of foreign investment.

(2) Case of Singapore

The FTA between the EU and Singapore is comprehensive. As mentioned above, it is composed of 17 chapters and contains a special chapter for investment, chapter 9 'investment protection'. Chapter 9 is composed of 30 articles and a special annex for the mediation mechanism for investor–State disputes as Annex 9-E. The Negotiations for a comprehensive free trade agreement between the EU and Singapore were launched in 2007, but the EU and Singapore finished the negotiations for a comprehensive FTA on 17 October 2014. It means that the FTA was drafted after the Treaty of Lisbon. Therefore, the exclusive competences in the field of direct investment are conferred on the EU and the commission negotiated investment issues profoundly and widely with Singapore.

(3) Case of Vietnam

The EU and the USA began to negotiate a Transatlantic Trade and Investment Partnership agreement (TTIP) in 2013. In negotiations it is considered as important for the EU to maintain or even emphasise the State's right to regulate, i.e. right to adopt generally binding laws for the purposes of health, environmental or consumer protection[8]. As the EU and the USA have had trade

---

[8] Cf. Commission document, Public consultation on modalities for investment protection and ISDS in TTIP, http://trade.ec.europa.eu/doclib/docs/2014/march/tradoc_152280.pdf.

conflicts regarding hormone-added meats and genetically modified organisms (GMO) based on the precautionary principle, European consumers and environmental non-governmental organisations (NGO) are very conscious about such matters. Facing that situation, the Commission published a proposal for investment protection and the investment court system for TTIP on 12 November 2015[9]. The compatibility of such a court with the autonomy of EU law is problematic according to the EU case law.

The FTA between the EU and Vietnam is also comprehensive. The negotiations for an FTA between the EU and Vietnam were launched in June 2012 after the Treaty of Lisbon. They finalized the FTA on 2 December 2015. It contains a special chapter for investment, chapter 8 'trade in services, investment and e-commerce'. Chapter 8 has seven subchapters, one of which, chapter II, is investment. Section 3 of Chapter II is resolution of investment disputes. Sub-Section 4 of Section 3 is investment tribunal system. It is composed of Articles 12~34. Article 12 is 'Tribunal' and Article 13 is 'Appeal Tribunal'. Thus, the FTA stipulates the establishment of a tribunal and an appeal tribunal. For the first time, the EU's FTA has such a tribunal system. Because of this, the FTA is meaningful and remarkable. Whether such an establishment of the tribunal would be compatible with EU law or how the tribunals will function should be seen.

(4) Case of Japan

Investment is a subject matter of the negotiations between the EU and Japan. However, the draft text or content of the negotiations are not published on the site of the EU and of the Japanese government.

---

[9] http://trade.ec.europa.eu/doclib/docs/2015/november/tradoc_153955.pdf.

2. *Geographical indication*

Intellectual property is an important subject matter of the FTAs by the EU. The EU did not have individual competence for intellectual property. However, the EU adopted a directive to approximate the laws of the Member States relating to trademark in 1988, based on Article 100 of an EEC Treaty (now, Article 114 TFEU)[10]. Further, the Council adopted a Regulation on the Community trademark, based on Article 235 EEC Treaty (now, Article 352 TFEU)[11]. As for the design, the Council adopted a regulation, based on Article 308 TEC (now, Article 352 TFEU) [12]. After the Treaty of Lisbon, the EU is given competences in the field of intellectual property in Article 118 TFEU and Article 207 TFEU.

One of the objectives of the FTA between the EU and South Korea is to adequately and effectively protect intellectual property rights (Article 1.1 (e)). Chapter 10 is a special chapter for intellectual property. Chapter 10 is composed of 69 Articles (Article 10.1 ~Article 10.69). Sub-section C covers geographical indication (GI) (Article 10.18~10.26). The FTA between the EU and Singapore also has a special chapter, chapter 11 (Article 11.1~11.52). The FTA has a special section for GI (subsection C), the protection of which is one of its objectives. 'A geographical indication (GI) is a sign used to indicate that a product has a specific geographical origin and possesses a certain reputation or qualities due to that place of origin'[13]. Footnote 14 of the FTA with Singapore explains that GI means an indication that identifies a good as originating in the territory

---

[10] OJ 1989 L 40/1, Council Directive 89/104/EEC of 21 December 1998 to approximate to the laws of the Member States relating to trade marks.

[11] OJ 1994 L11/1, Council Regulation No 40/94 of 20 December 1993 on the Community trade mark.

[12] OJ 2002 L3/1, Council Regulation 6/2002 of 12 December 2001 on Community designs.

[13] http://ec.europa.eu/growth/industry/intellectual-property/geographical-indications/non-agricultural-products/index_en.htm.

of a Party, or a region or locality in that territory, where a given quality, reputation or other characteristic of the good is essentially attributable to its geographical origin.

The FTA between the EU and Vietnam contains a special chapter, i.e. chapter 12 for intellectual property. GI is also one of the objectives of intellectual property. Article 6.1~Article 6.11 are designed for GI. Provisional 'Annex GI-1' lists GIs of the EU and Vietnam. 'Franken' Wine, 'Prosiutto di Parma' Ham, 'Gauda Holland' Cheese are three of the 171 GIs for the EU. 'Vinh' Orange, 'Mộc Châo' Tea, 'Trùng Khánh' Chestnut are three of the 38 GIs for Vietnam.

Japan is negotiating an FTA with the EU. The EU's interests are 1) Japan's Non-Tariff Measures (NTMs) on autos, drugs, medical devices, food safety and processed food, 2) public procurement (particularly market access to railways, electricity and gas) and 3) geographical indication (GI). For the EU, GI is one of the FTA's most important subjects. During the negotiations, the Japanese government felt this pressure and at the same time recognized the importance of GI. Therefore, the Act of Protection of Names of Designated Agricultural, Forestry and Fishery Products and Foodstuffs (Geographical Indication Act) was enforced in Japan in June 2015.

3. Environment

At the EEC's establishment in 1958, the TEEC did not cover environmental issues because its primary focus was economic integration[14]. At the 1972 Paris summit, heads of state or governments of the Member States agreed that the Community should take measures to protect the environment. After the Single European Act (SEA) of 1987, competences in the field of environment were given to the EU

---

[14] Yumiko Nakanishi, 'Introduction: The Impact of the International and European Union Environmental Law on Japanese Basic Environmental Law', ders., *Contemporary Issues in Environmental Law-the EU and Japan-*, Springer, 2016, pp. 2-4.

(Article 130t TEEC, now, Article 192 TFEU). The Rio Summit (of the United Nations Conference on Environment and Development, UNEP) was held in 1992, and after that, the concept of 'sustainable growth' was introduced in the EU by the Treaty of Maastricht, 1993. Furthermore, the 1997 Treaty of Amsterdam introduced the concept 'sustainable development' and subsequently became a key concept of the EU. Sustainable development is now one of the important objectives of the EU's external policies (Article 21 TEU).

The Preamble of the FTA between the EU and South Korea mentions the commitment to sustainable development and the development and enforcement of environmental laws and policies. Article 1.1 paragraph 2 (g) establishes that one of the objectives is 'to commit, in the recognition that sustainable development is an overarching objective, to the development of international trade in such a way so as to contribute to the objective of sustainable development'. Chapter 13 of the FTA is 'trade and sustainable development' (Article 13.1 13.16). The FTA is primarily a trade agreement, but it also establishes the Parties' commitment to promote the development of international trade in such a way so as to contribute to the objective of sustainable development and to ensure that this objective should be integrated and reflected at every level of their trade relationship (Article 13.1 paragraph 1). The latter part reflects the principle of environmental integration in Article 11 TFEU[15]. Article 5.1 (2) encourages cooperation on animal welfare issues while Article 5.9 establishes that the Parties shall cooperate in the development of animal welfare standards in international fora, in particular with respect to the stunning and slaughter of animals. It reflects Article 13 TFEU's focus on animal welfare.

Chapter 13 of the FTA between the EU and Singapore rules trade

---

[15] Article 11 TFEU rules, 'Environmental protection requirements must be integrated into the definition and implementation of the Union's policies and activities, in particular with a view to promoting sustainable development'.

and sustainable development (Article 13.1-13.17). According to Article 13.6 paragraph 1, as a response of the international community to global or regional environmental problems, the Parties recognise the value of international environmental governance and agreements. Article 13.11 emphasizes the importance of facilitating and promoting investment to protect the environment. Further, it is remarkable that the FTA lays down an establishment of a monitoring mechanism for implementing the chapter.

The FTA between the EU and Vietnam stipulates a chapter for trade and sustainable development, Chapter 15 (Article 1-17). It also sets forth an 'institutional set-up and overseeing mechanism' in Article 15.

The EU is keen to raise the standard of environmental protection through trade and investment agreements with third countries. In addition, the concept of sustainable development includes not only environmental development but also social development. It is considered as a kind of soft pressure from the EU toward third world countries.

V. FTAs and political principles

In the preamble of the FTA between the EU and South Korea, the parties reaffirm their commitment to the Universal Declaration of Human Rights adopted by the General Assembly of the United Nations on 10 December 1948 as well as their desire to strengthen the development and enforcement of labour laws and polices and promote basic workers' rights and sustainable development and implement the agreement in a manner consistent with the objectives. The preambles of the FTAs between the EU and Singapore and between the EU and Vietnam also refer to the same Universal Declaration. It means that trade and human rights are connected to each other and reflect a strategic policy of the EU.

After the Treaty of Lisbon in 2009, Article 21 of the Treaty on the European Union (TEU) stipulates the supposed political principles concerning human rights, democracy and rule of law[16]. Therefore, the EU eagerly pushes a conclusion of binding political agreements that set forth political principles. The EU concluded a Framework Agreement with South Korea[17]. The framework agreement is a comprehensive agreement that includes political elements. The EU concluded a Partnership and Cooperation Agreement (PCA) with Singapore[18]. The EU concluded a new Partnership and Cooperation Agreement with Vietnam on 27 June 2012. The EU and Thailand have negotiated and initialled a Partnership and Cooperation Agreement, but it is not signed by the EU and its Member States because a democratically elected government is not in place[19]. The EU is negotiating a Partnership and Cooperation Agreement with Malaysia. The EU requested Japan to conclude a political agreement and now the EU and Japan are negotiating a strategic partnership agreement alongside the FTA. Asian countries that have concluded or are negotiating FTAs should also conclude political agreements with the EU (Partnership and Cooperation Agreement or strategic partnership agreement). The application of political principles could be a means of normative power[20].

Article 1 paragraph 1 of the Framework Agreement between the EU and South Korea states that respect for democratic principles, human rights and fundamental freedoms as enumerated in the Universal Declaration of Human Rights and other relevant international human

---

[16] Yumiko Nakanishi, 'Political Principles in Article 21 TEU and Constitutionalism', Hitotsubashi Journal of Law and Politics, Vol 42, pp. 11-23; http://hermes-ir.lib.hit-u.ac.jp/rs/bitstream/10086/26442/1/HJlaw0420000110.pdf.

[17] http://eeas.europa.eu/korea_south/docs/framework_agreement_final_en.pdf.

[18] http://eeas.europa.eu/statements/docs/2013/131014_02_en.pdf.

[19] http://eeas.europa.eu/thailand/index_en.htm.

[20] Cf. Henri de Waele, Layered Global Player, 2011, Springer, p. 96; Cf. Gráinne de Búrca, 'EU External Relations: The Governance Mode of Foreign Policy', in Bart Van Vooren/Steven Blockmans/Jan Wouters (ed.), *The EU's Role in Global Governance*, 2013, Oxford University Press, p. 39, p. 40.

rights instruments constitutes an essential element of this Agreement. On the other hand, Article 45 paragraph 3 is the alleged non-compliance clause. If Asian countries do not comply with their political agreement, the EU will stop application of the FTA. An FTA and a political agreement form a set not only in the negotiation stage but also in the implementation stage. This is a type of 'carrot and stick' approach.

The Commission published a working document regarding the PCA with Vietnam in January 2016[21]. According to the document, PCAs are manifestation of the EU's commitment to building a predictable, rule-based international order[22]. It is said that in line with Article 21 TEU and Article 207 TFEU, the EU pursues an integrated approach to the protection of human rights in the context of its trade policy, including FTAs[23], thus connecting FTAs with human rights[24].

VI. Conclusion

After the Treaty of Lisbon, the division of competences between the EU and its Member States changed, particularly in the field of common commercial policy. The EEAS was established and the EU's value and political principles were explicitly set forth.

As explained above, the EU has concluded or is negotiating FTAs with Asian countries. Those FTAs have much in common. First, they are no longer simply 'trade' agreements but are more comprehensive. Secondly, FTAs now concern investment, intellectual property (GI) and sustainable development, which are in the EU's interest. Thirdly, the EU

---

[21] SWD (2016) 21, Human Rights and Sustainable Development in the EU-Vietnam Relations with specific regard to the EU-Vietnam Free Trade Agreement.

[22] Ibid., p. 3.

[23] Ibid., p. 7.

[24] Ibid., p. 16.

is keen to conclude political agreements (PCAs) alongside the FTAs. Fourthly, human rights and sustainable development are integrated in the EU's trade policy. After the Treaty of Lisbon, the EU established the European External Action Service (EEAS) to support its foreign policy. In addition, the EU has its own political principles in external actions (Article 21 TEU).

The FTAs between the EU and Asian countries can be discussed in the global context, while considering an FTA with Canada, i.e. Comprehensive Economic and Trade Agreement (CETA), TTIP and other FTAs. The negotiations and texts of agreements have influenced each other. For example, the FTA between the EU and Singapore does not include an investment tribunal. The draft regarding investment of TTIP includes both the investment tribunal and appeal tribunal. It influenced the FTA between the EU and Vietnam. The FTA with Vietnam establishes the investment tribunal and appeal tribunal. It influenced the CETA. Trans-Pacific Partnership Agreement (TPP) was signed by 12 countries including Singapore, Brunei, Vietnam, Malaysia and Japan on 4 February 2016. The negotiations of those mega-FTAs are conducted in parallel and influenced each other.

Further, Asian countries have negotiated or are negotiating FTAs with the European Commission and among Asian countries. The contents of FTAs are becoming similar. Shared experience of Asian countries through negotiations with the European Commission might be useful to build a strategy for relations with the EU. Additionally, those experiences might contribute to the development of protection of human rights and the environment in Asian countries to some extent.

The FTAs developed rapidly and are developing after countries realized that it was difficult to proceed in the framework of the WTO. If we consider the number and contents of the FTAs in the world, we cannot ignore their importance. The EU's strategy changed a great deal after the Treaty of Lisbon: FTAs became more comprehensive and the

EU's competences changed as well. The FTAs between the EU and Asian countries are still nascent and merit careful future observation.

TTIP, ISDS, and Foreign Investment Court

Dr. Catherine Li

Professor of Department of Law, Soochow University

I. Introduction

The filed claims for Investor-State Dispute Settlement (ISDS) has increased over the past few years, the number has been sharply rising, especially in the past ten years.[1] Correlatively, there are more and more reflections about the ISDS mechanism and its pros and cons. Indeed, there are some problems and reforms which have been discussed. According to the European Union's Free Trade Agreement with Vietnam and Canada (Comprehensive Economic and Trade Agreement, CETA), the Contracting Parties has agreed a new mechanism for the investment disputes, i.e. the foreign investment court system. Recently, the European Union and the United States have been negotiating on the Transatlantic Trade and Investment Partnership (TTIP) terms, the European Commission in its text proposal, also brings up the investment court system for resolving disputes between investors and states.[2] Accordingly, this article is going to discuss the problems of the ISDS and the background of setting up a foreign investment court system, then

---

[1] United Nations Conference on Trade and Development, *World Investment Report*, 2013, at 110-111.

[2] European Commission - Press release, http://europa.eu/rapid/press-release_IP-15-5651_en.htm (last visited April 12, 2016).

comparing the relevant articles between the CETA and the draft articles of the TTIP.

II. Why setting up the Investment Court System?

1. *The problems of the ISDS mechanism*

As mentioned above, the ISDS mechanism has several concerns which have been long existed. In 2013 World Investment Report of the United Nations Conference on Trade and Development (UNCTAD), it referred several issues. The first problem is legitimacy, in other words, whether the ad hoc arbitrators, when the cases involve public policy issues, can be reliable.[3] The second concern is transparency which is that the ISDS proceedings are kept confidential if the dispute parties wanted or even the cases involves public matters.[4] The third is the consistency of arbitral decisions and erroneous decisions. These two concerns mean that different arbitral tribunal has different standard and interpretation which led to inconsistent findings, and if there are substantive mistakes made by arbitral tribunal, in the current mechanism, it can't be corrected.[5] The final is that the arbitrator's independence and impartiality issue.[6] Consequently, the report referred some of the reforms including introducing an appeals facility and creating an international investment court.[7]

Through introducing an appeals facility, it can be seen as a means to improve the consistency of the findings, correcting erroneous decisions

---

[3] *Supra* 1, at 112.

[4] *Id.*

[5] *Id.*

[6] *Id.*

[7] *Id.*

of first tribunals, unifying the interpretation of the law and enhancing its predictability. Besides, it would add order and direction to the existing ad hoc regime.[8] Furthermore, establishing a standing international investment court could resolve most of the above problems, it could ensure the legitimacy and the transparency of the systems, and facilitate consistency and accuracy of the decisions, and the independence and impartiality of the judges.[9]

2. *The Role of the European Union and its Member States*

Under the Lisbon Treaty, Article 207 establishes for the first time an exclusive competence over foreign investment by including it in the scope of the Common Commercial Policy. Nevertheless, the scope of application of the EU foreign investment policy is not yet clear. However, it can be inferred that the European Union has the competence to negotiate the terms of investor-state dispute, or even the condition of expropriation.[10] Therefore, after the Lisbon Treaty entered into force, the competence for foreign direct investment has transferred to EU level. Basically, member states cannot conclude bilateral investment agreements on its own behalf which belongs to the EU competence.

Nevertheless, according to article 25of the ICSID Convention, it states that the dispute parties are contracting state (or any constituent subdivision or agency of a Contracting State designated to the Centre by that State) and a national of another Contracting State, and national of another contracting state means natural person and juridical person.[11]

In sum, because the ISDS dispute parties are limited to investors

---

[8] *Id.* at 115.

[9] *Id.* at 116.

[10] Catherine Li, *The Legal Norms on the European Union's International Investment Policy*, vol.42 no.2, A Journal of European and American Studies 339, 2012, at 345.

[11] *Id.* at 346-47.

and states, it is an awkward situation for European Union. It has to find solutions to adapt the new structure, otherwise it will go backward that if there is any dispute concerning investment activities, European Union can only rely on its member states to submit the claims.

III. The Articles of the CETA and the TTIP

This section would focus on the issues which the UNCTAD World Investment Report has mentioned, and introducing the relevant regulations of the CETA[12] and TTIP[13], as well as comparing the difference. The section includes mainly about the composition of tribunal, the appellate tribunal, ethics, applicable rules and interpretation, and transparency.

1. The composition of the tribunal

TTIP	CETA
➢ Chapter 2, Sub-section 4, Article 9	➢ Chapter 8, Section F, Article 8.27
1. A Tribunal of First Instance ('Tribunal') is hereby established to hear claims submitted pursuant to Article 6.	1. The Tribunal established under this Section shall decide claims submitted pursuant to Article 8.23.
2. The [...] Committee shall, upon the entry into	2. The CETA Joint Committee shall, upon the entry into force of this Agreement,

---

[12] Comprehensive Economic and Trade Agreement, http://trade.ec.europa.eu/doclib/docs/2014/september/tradoc_152806.pdf, last visited April 12, 2016.

[13] EU textual proposal of Transatlantic Trade and Investment Partnership, http://trade.ec.europa.eu/doclib/docs/2015/november/tradoc_153955.pdf, last visited April 12, 2016.

force of this Agreement, appoint <u>fifteen Judges to the Tribunal</u>. Five of the Judges shall be nationals of a Member State of the European Union, five shall be nationals of the United States and five shall be nationals of third countries.

3. The [...] Committee may decide to increase or to decrease the number of the Judges by multiples of three. Additional appointments shall be made on the same basis as provided for in paragraph 2.

4. The Judges shall possess the qualifications required in their respective countries for appointment to judicial office, or be jurists of recognized competence. They shall have demonstrated expertise in public international law. <u>It is desirable that they have expertise in particular, in international investment law, international trade law and</u>

appoint <u>fifteen Members of the Tribunal</u>. Five of the Members of the Tribunal shall be nationals of a Member State of the European Union, five shall be nationals of Canada and five shall be nationals of third countries.

3. The CETA Joint Committee may decide to increase or to decrease the number of the Members of the Tribunal by multiples of three. Additional appointments shall be made on the same basis as provided for in paragraph 2.

4. The Members of the Tribunal shall possess the qualifications required in their respective countries for appointment to judicial office, or be jurists of recognized competence. <u>They shall have demonstrated expertise in public international law. It is desirable that they have expertise in particular, in</u>

the resolution of disputes arising under international investment or international trade agreements.

5. The Judges appointed pursuant to this Section shall be appointed for a **six-year term**, renewable once. However, the terms of seven of the fifteen persons appointed immediately after the entry into force of the Agreement, to be determined by lot, shall extend to **nine years**. Vacancies shall be filled as they arise. A person appointed to replace a person whose term of office has not expired shall hold office for the remainder of the predecessor's term.

6. The Tribunal shall hear cases in divisions consisting of three Judges, of whom one shall be a national of a Member State of the European Union, one a national of the United States and one a national of a third country. The division shall

international investment law, in international trade law and the resolution of disputes arising under international investment or international trade agreements.

5. The Members of the Tribunal appointed pursuant to this Section shall be appointed for a **five-year term**, renewable once. However, the terms of seven of the 15 persons appointed immediately after the entry into force of the Agreement, to be determined by lot, shall extend to **six years**. Vacancies shall be filled as they arise. A person appointed to replace a Member of the Tribunal whose term of office has not expired shall hold office for the remainder of the predecessor's term. In principle, a Member of the Tribunal serving on a division of the Tribunal when his or her term expires

be chaired by the Judge who is a national of a third country.

7. Within 90 days of the submission of a claim pursuant to Article 6, the President of the Tribunal shall appoint the Judges composing the division of the Tribunal hearing the case on a rotation basis, ensuring that the composition of the divisions is random and unpredictable, while giving equal opportunity to all Judges to serve.

8. The President and Vice-President of the Tribunal shall be responsible for organizational issues and will be appointed for a two-year term and shall be drawn by lot from among the Judges who are nationals of third countries. They shall serve on the basis of a rotation drawn by lot by the Chair of the [..] Committee. The Vice-President shall replace the President when the

may continue to serve on the division until a final award is issued.

6. The Tribunal shall hear cases in divisions consisting of three Members of the Tribunal, of whom one shall be a national of a Member State of the European Union, one a national of Canada and one a national of a third country. The division shall be chaired by the Member of the Tribunal who is a national of a third country.

7. Within 90 days of the submission of a claim pursuant to Article 8.23, the President of the Tribunal shall appoint the Members of the Tribunal composing the division of the Tribunal hearing the case on a rotation basis, ensuring that the composition of the divisions is random and unpredictable, while giving equal opportunity to all Members of the Tribunal to

President is unavailable.

9. Notwithstanding paragraph 6, the disputing parties may agree that a case be heard by a sole Judge who is a national of a third country, to be selected by the President of the Tribunal. The respondent shall give sympathetic consideration to such a request from the claimant, in particular where the claimant is a small or medium-sized enterprise or the compensation or damages claimed are relatively low. Such a request should be made at the same time as the filing of the claim pursuant to Article 6.

10. The Tribunal shall draw up its own working procedures.

11. The Judges shall be available at all times and on short notice, and shall stay abreast of dispute settlement activities under this Agreement.

12. In order to ensure their availability, the Judges shall

serve.

8. The President and Vice-President of the Tribunal shall be responsible for organizational issues and will be appointed for a two-year term and shall be drawn by lot from among the Members of the Tribunal who are nationals of third countries. They shall serve on the basis of a rotation drawn by lot by the Chair of the CETA Joint Committee. The Vice-President shall replace the President when the President is unavailable.

9. Notwithstanding paragraph 6, the disputing parties may agree that a case be heard by a sole Member of the Tribunal to be appointed at random from the third country nationals. The respondent shall give sympathetic consideration to a request from the claimant to have the case heard by a sole Member of the Tribunal, in particular where the claimant

be paid a monthly retainer fee to be fixed by decision of the [...] Committee. [Note: the retainer fee suggested by the EU would be around 1/3rd of the retainer fee for WTO Appellate Body members (i.e. around € 2,000 per month)] The President of the Tribunal and, where applicable, the Vice-President, shall receive a fee equivalent to the fee determined pursuant to Article 10(12) for each day worked in fulfilling the functions of President of the Tribunal pursuant to this Section.

13. The retainer fee shall be paid equally by both Parties into an account managed by the Secretariat of [ICSID/ the Permanent Court of Arbitration]. In the event that one Party fails to pay the retainer fee the other Party may elect to pay. Any such arrears will remain payable, with appropriate

is a small or medium-sized enterprise or the compensation or damages claimed are relatively low. Such a request shall be made before the constitution of the division of the Tribunal.

10. The Tribunal may draw up its own working procedures.

11. The Members of the Tribunal shall ensure that they are available and able to perform the functions set out under this Section.

12. In order to ensure their availability, the Members of the Tribunal shall be paid a monthly retainer fee to be determined by the CETA Joint Committee.

13. The fees referred to in paragraph 12 shall be paid equally by both Parties into an account managed by the ICSID Secretariat. In the event that one Party fails to pay the retainer fee the other Party may elect to pay. Any such arrears by a Party will remain payable, with

interest.

14. Unless the [..] Committee adopts a decision pursuant to paragraph 15, the amount of the other fees and expenses of the Judges on a division of the Investment Tribunal shall be those determined pursuant to Regulation 14(1) of the Administrative and Financial Regulations of the ICSID Convention in force on the date of the submission of the claim and allocated by the Tribunal among the disputing parties in accordance with Article 28(4).

15. Upon a decision by the [...] Committee, the retainer fee and other fees and expenses may be permanently transformed into a regular salary. In such an event, the Judges shall serve on a full-time basis and the [...] Committee shall fix their remuneration and related organizational matters. In that event, the Judges shall

appropriate interest.

14. Unless the CETA Joint Committee adopts a decision pursuant to paragraph 15, the amount of the fees and expenses of the Members of the Tribunal on a division constituted to hear a claim, other than the fees referred to in paragraph 12, shall be those determined pursuant to Regulation 14(1) of the Administrative and Financial Regulations of the ICSID Convention in force on the date of the submission of the claim and allocated by the Tribunal among the disputing parties in accordance with Article 8.39.5.

not be permitted to engage in any occupation, whether gainful or not, unless exemption is exceptionally granted by the President of the Tribunal. 16. The Secretariat of [ICSID/ the Permanent Court of Arbitration] shall act as Secretariat for the Tribunal and provide it with appropriate support. The expenses for such support shall be met by the Parties to the Agreement equally.	

As shown above, in TTIP Chapter 2, Sub-section 4, Article 9 and CETA Chapter 8, Section F, Article 8.27, they regulate the composition of the tribunal mainly about the numbers of the tribunal, term of office, and the qualification. They are mostly the same; however, in the term of the tribunal, TTIP and CETA have different position.

2. *The appellate tribunal*

TTIP	CETA
➤ Article 10 1. A permanent Appeal Tribunal is hereby established to hear appeals from the awards issued by	➤ Article 8.28 1. An Appellate Tribunal is hereby established to review awards rendered under this Section.

the Tribunal.

2. The Appeal Tribunal shall be composed of six Members, of whom two shall be nationals of a Member State of the European Union, two shall be nationals of the United States and two shall be nationals of third countries.

3. The Parties, by decision of the [...] Committee, shall, upon the entry into force of this Agreement, appoint the members of the Appeal Tribunal. For this purpose, each Party shall propose three candidates, two of which may be nationals of that Party and one shall be a non-national, for the [...] Committee to thereafter jointly appoint the Members.

4. The Committee may agree to increase the number of the Members of the Appeal Tribunal by multiples of three. Additional appointments shall be made

2. The Appellate Tribunal may uphold, modify or reverse a Tribunal's award based on:

(a) errors in the application or interpretation of applicable law;

(b) manifest errors in the appreciation of the facts, including the appreciation of relevant domestic law;

(c) the grounds set out in Article 52(1) (a) through (e) of the ICSID Convention, in so far as they are not covered by paragraphs (a) and (b).

3. The Members of the Appellate Tribunal shall be appointed by a decision of the CETA Joint Committee at the same time as the decision referred to in paragraph 7.

4. The Members of the Appellate Tribunal shall meet the requirements of Articles 8.27.4 and comply with Article 8.30.

5. The division of the Appellate Tribunal constituted to hear

on the same basis as provided for in paragraph 3.

5. The Appeal Tribunal Members shall be appointed for a six-year term, renewable once. However, the terms of three of the six persons appointed immediately after the entry into force of the agreement, to be determined by lot, shall extend to nine years. Vacancies shall be filled as they arise. A person appointed to replace a person whose term of office has not expired shall hold office for the remainder of the predecessor's term.

6. The Appeal Tribunal shall have a President and Vice-President who shall be selected by lot for a two-year term and shall be selected from among the Members who are nationals of third countries. They shall serve on the basis of a rotation drawn by lot by the Chair of the [..] Committee. The Vice-President shall replace the appeal shall consist of three randomly appointed Members of the Appellate Tribunal.

6. Articles 8.36 and 8.38 shall apply to the proceedings before the Appellate Tribunal.

7. The CETA Joint Committee shall promptly adopt a decision setting out the following administrative and organizational matters regarding the functioning of the Appellate Tribunal:

(a) administrative support;

(b) procedures for the initiation and the conduct of appeals, and procedures for referring issues back to the Tribunal for adjustment of the award, as appropriate;

(c) procedures for filling a vacancy on the Appellate Tribunal and on a division of the Appellate Tribunal constituted to hear a case;

(d) remuneration of the Members of the Appellate Tribunal;

the President when the President is unavailable.

7. The Members of the Appeal Tribunal shall possess the qualifications required in their respective countries for appointment to the highest judicial offices, or be jurists of recognized competence. They shall have demonstrated expertise in public international law. It is desirable that they have expertise in international investment law, international trade law and the resolution of disputes arising under international investment or international trade agreements.

8. The Appeal Tribunal shall hear appeals in divisions consisting of three Members. The division shall be chaired by the Member who is a national of a third country.

9. The composition of the division hearing each appeal shall be established in each

(e) provisions related to the costs of appeals;

(f) the number of Members of the Appellate Tribunal; and

(g) any other elements it determines to be necessary for the effective functioning of the Appellate Tribunal.

8. The Committee on Services and Investment shall periodically review the functioning of the Appellate Tribunal and may make recommendations to the CETA Joint Committee. The CETA Joint Committee may revise the decision referred to in paragraph 7, if necessary.

9. Upon adoption of the decision referred to in paragraph 7:

(a) a disputing party may appeal an award rendered pursuant to this Section to the Appellate Tribunal within 90 days after its issuance;

(b) a disputing party shall not seek to review, set aside,

case by the President of the Appeal Tribunal on a rotation basis, ensuring that the composition of each division is random and unpredictable, while giving equal opportunity to all Members to serve.

10. The Appeal Tribunal shall draw up its own working procedures.

11. All persons serving on the Appeal Tribunal shall be available at all times and on short notice and shall stay abreast of other dispute settlement activities under this agreement.

12. The Members of the Appeal Tribunal shall be paid a monthly retainer fee and receive a fee for each day worked as a Member, to be determined by decision of the [...] Committee. [Note: the retainer and daily fee suggested by the EU would be around the same as for WTO Appeal Tribunal members (i.e. a retainer fee

annul, revise or initiate any other similar procedure as regards an award under this Section;

(c) an award rendered pursuant to Article 8.39 shall not be considered final and no action for enforcement of an award may be brought until either:

(i) 90 days from the issuance of the award by the Tribunal has elapsed and no appeal has been initiated;

(ii) an initiated appeal has been rejected or withdrawn; or

(iii) 90 days have elapsed from an award by the Appellate Tribunal and the Appellate Tribunal has not referred the matter back to the Tribunal;

(d) a final award by the Appellate Tribunal shall be considered as a final award for the purposes of Article 8.41; and

(e) Article 8.41.3 shall not apply.

of around € 7,000 per
month)].

13. The remuneration of the
Members shall be paid
equally by both Parties into
an account managed by
the Secretariat of [ICSID/
the Permanent Court of
Arbitration]. In the event
that one Party fails to pay
the retainer fee the other
Party may elect to pay. Any
such arrears will remain
payable, with appropriate
interest

14. Upon a decision by the [...]
Committee, the retainer
fee and the fees for days
worked may be permanently
transformed into a regular
salary. In such an event,
the Members of the Appeal
Tribunal shall serve on a
full-time basis and the [...]
Committee shall fix their
remuneration and related
organizational matters. In
that event, the Members
shall not be permitted to
engage in any

occupation, whether gainful or not, unless exemption is exceptionally granted by the President of the Appeal Tribunal. 15. The Secretariat [ICSID/ the Permanent Court of Arbitration] shall act as Secretariat for the Appeal Tribunal and provide it with appropriate support. The expenses for such support shall be met by the Parties to the Agreement equally.	

In the appellate tribunal, the CETA doesn't make a clear position about the number of the tribunal, the term, and the qualification of the members; it only relies on a decision of the CETA Joint Committee. On the contrary, TTIP makes it clear, in similarity of the article about the composition of the first instance tribunal; it provides the number, term and the qualification of the appellate tribunal.

3. *Ethics*

TTIP	CETA
➢ Article 11 1. The Judges of the Tribunal and the Members of the Appeal Tribunal shall be chosen from persons	➢ Article 8.30 1. The Members of the Tribunal shall be <u>independent</u>. They shall not be affiliated with any government. They shall

whose <u>independence</u> is beyond doubt. They shall not be affiliated with any government. They shall not take instructions from any government or organization with regard to matters related to the dispute. They shall not participate in the consideration of any disputes that would create a direct or indirect conflict of interest. In so doing they shall comply with Annex II (Code of Conduct). In addition, upon appointment, they shall refrain from acting as counsel in any pending or new investment protection dispute under this or any other agreement or domestic law.

2. If a disputing party considers that a Judge or a Member has conflict of interest, it shall send a notice of challenge to the appointment to the President of the Tribunal or to the President of the Appeal Tribunal, respectively.

not take instructions from any organization, or government with regard to matters related to the dispute. They shall not participate in the consideration of any disputes that would create a direct or indirect conflict of interest. They shall comply with the International Bar Association Guidelines on Conflicts of Interest in International Arbitration or any supplemental rules adopted pursuant to Article 8.44.2. In addition, upon appointment, they shall refrain from acting as counsel or as party-appointed expert or witness in any pending or new investment dispute under this or any other international agreement.

2. If a disputing party considers that a Member of the Tribunal has a conflict of interest, it shall send to the President of the International Court of Justice a notice of challenge to the

The notice of challenge shall be sent within 15 days of the date on which the composition of the division of the Tribunal or of the Appeal Tribunal has been communicated to the disputing party, or within 15 days of the date on which the relevant facts came to its knowledge, if they could not have reasonably been known at the time of composition of the division. The notice of challenge shall state the grounds for the challenge.

3. If, within 15 days from the date of the notice of challenge, the challenged Judge or Member has elected not to resign from that division, the President of the Tribunal or the President of the Appeal Tribunal, respectively, shall, after hearing the disputing parties and after providing the Judge or the Member an opportunity to submit any observations, issue a decision

appointment. The notice of challenge shall be sent within 15 days of the date on which the composition of the division of the Tribunal has been communicated to the disputing party, or within 15 days of the date on which the relevant facts came to its knowledge, if they could not have reasonably been known at the time of composition of the division. The notice of challenge shall state the grounds for the challenge.

3. If, within 15 days from the date of the notice of challenge, the challenged Member of the Tribunal has elected not to resign from the division, the President of the International Court of Justice shall, after hearing the disputing parties and after providing the Member of the Tribunal an opportunity to submit any observations, issue a decision within 45 days of receipt of the notice of challenge and notify

within 45 days of receipt of the notice of challenge and forthwith notify the disputing parties and other Judges or Members of the division.	the disputing parties and the other Members of the division. A vacancy resulting from the disqualification or resignation of a Member of the Tribunal shall be filled promptly.
4. Challenges against the appointment to a division of the President of the Tribunal shall be decided by the President of the Appeal Tribunal and vice-versa.	4. Upon a reasoned recommendation from the President of the Tribunal, or on their joint initiative, the Parties, by decision of the CETA Joint Committee, may remove a Member from the Tribunal where his or her behaviour is inconsistent with the obligations set out in paragraph 1 and incompatible with his or her continued membership of the Tribunal.

The most important thing about the member or judge of the tribunal is the independence. These articles can avoid the problems of the ISDS mechanism that because arbitrators on ISDS tribunals are chosen by the disputing parties, they may be influenced by the disputes parties. Besides, there are code of conducts for the members of the tribunal in TTIP Annex II, and CETA Annex 29-B.

4. Applicable rules and interpretation

TTIP	CETA
➤ Article 13	➤ Article 8.31
1. The Tribunal shall determine whether the treatment subject to the claim is inconsistent with any of the provisions referred to in Article 1(1) alleged by the claimant.	1. When rendering its decision, the Tribunal established under this Section shall apply this Agreement as interpreted in accordance with the Vienna Convention on the Law of Treaties, and other rules and principles of international law applicable between the Parties.
2. In making its determination, the Tribunal shall apply the provisions of this Agreement and other rules of international law applicable between the Parties. It shall interpret this Agreement in accordance with customary rules of interpretation of public international law, as codified in the Vienna Convention on the Law of Treaties.	2. The Tribunal shall not have jurisdiction to determine the legality of a measure, alleged to constitute a breach of this Agreement, under the domestic law of the disputing Party. For greater certainty, in determining the consistency of a measure with this Agreement, the Tribunal may consider, as appropriate, the domestic law of the disputing Party as a matter of fact. In doing so, the Tribunal shall follow the prevailing interpretation
3. For greater certainty, pursuant to paragraph 1, the domestic law of the Parties shall not be part of the applicable law. Where the Tribunal is required to	

ascertain the meaning of a provision of the domestic law of one of the Parties as a matter of fact, it shall follow the prevailing interpretation of that provision made by the courts or authorities of that Party.

4. For greater certainty, the meaning given to the relevant domestic law made by the Tribunal shall not be binding upon the courts or the authorities of either Party. The Tribunal shall not have jurisdiction to determine the legality of a measure, alleged to constitute a breach of this Agreement, under the domestic law of the disputing Party.

5. Where serious concerns arise as regards matters of interpretation relating to [the Investment Protection or the Resolution of Investment Disputes and Investment Court System Section of this Agreement],

given to the domestic law by the courts or authorities of that Party and any meaning given to domestic law by the Tribunal shall not be binding upon the courts or the authorities of that Party.

3. Where serious concerns arise as regards matters of interpretation that may affect investment, the Committee on Services and Investment may, pursuant to Article 8.44.3(a), recommend to the CETA Joint Committee the adoption of interpretations of this Agreement. An interpretation adopted by the CETA Joint Committee shall be binding on a Tribunal established under this Section. The CETA Joint Committee may decide that an interpretation shall have binding effect from a specific date.

the [] Committee may adopt decisions interpreting those provisions. Any such interpretation shall be binding on the Tribunal and the Appeal Tribunal. The [] Committee may decide that an interpretation shall have binding effect from a specific date.	

5. *Transparency*

TTIP	CETA
➤ Article 18 1. The "UNCITRAL Transparency Rules" shall apply to disputes under this Section, with the following additional obligations. 2. The request for consultations under Article 4, the request for a determination and the notice of determination under Article 5, the agreement to mediate under Article 3, the notice of challenge and the decision on challenge under Article 11 the request for	➤ Article 8.36 1. The UNCITRAL Transparency Rules, as modified by this Chapter, shall apply in connection with proceedings under this Section. 2. The request for consultations, the notice requesting a determination of the respondent, the notice of determination of the respondent, the agreement to mediate, the notice of intent to challenge a Member of the Tribunal, the

consolidation under Article 27 and all document submitted to and issued by the Appeal Tribunal shall be included in the list of documents referred to in Article 3(1) of the UNCITRAL Transparency Rules.

3. Exhibits shall be included in the list of documents mentioned in Article 3(2) of the UNCITRAL Transparency Rules.

4. Notwithstanding Article 2 of the UNCITRAL Transparency Rules, the European Union or the United States as the case may be shall make publicly available in a timely manner prior to the constitution of the division, relevant documents pursuant to paragraph 2, subject to the redaction of confidential or protected information. Such documents may be made publicly available by communication to

decision on challenge to a Member of the Tribunal and the request for consolidation shall be included in the list of documents to be made available to the public under Article 3(1) of the UNCITRAL Transparency Rules.

3. Exhibits shall be included in the list of documents to be made available to the public under Article 3(2) of the UNCITRAL Transparency Rules.

4. Notwithstanding Article 2 of the UNCITRAL Transparency Rules, prior to the constitution of the Tribunal, Canada or the European Union as the case may be shall make publicly available in a timely manner relevant documents pursuant to paragraph 2, subject to the redaction of confidential or protected information. Such documents may be made publicly available by communication to the

the repository referred to in the UNCITRAL Transparency Rules.

5. A disputing party may disclose to other persons in connection with proceedings, including witnesses and experts, such unredacted documents as it considers necessary in the course of proceedings under this Section. However, the disputing party shall ensure that those persons protect the confidential or protected information in those documents.

repository.

5. Hearings shall be open to the public. The Tribunal shall determine, in consultation with the disputing parties, the appropriate logistical arrangements to facilitate public access to such hearings. If the Tribunal determines that there is a need to protect confidential or protected information, it shall make the appropriate arrangements to hold in private that part of the hearing requiring such protection.

6. Nothing in this Chapter requires a respondent to withhold from the public information required to be disclosed by its laws. The respondent should apply those laws in a manner sensitive to protecting from disclosure information that has been designated as confidential or protected information.

IV. Conclusion

It is very obvious that the European Union wishes to set up a new model for the investment disputes settlement. The EU tries to make several improvements on the issues which ISDS mechanism has long been criticized, especially the appellate tribunal system. It is said that the CETA would be the reference of the TTIP negotiations, and we should wait and see whether the United States would accept the investment court system until the latter round of negotiation. However, the investment court system can be regarded as the reformation of the current system. As for the CETA and EU-Vietnam free trade agreements have taken the lead, the investment court system is not enforceable. Considering the United States and the European Union play the important role of international economic activities, it is a chance to set up new rules. For better or worse, whether the investment court system is better than current ISDS mechanism, time has its say.

The Impact of the EU-Korea FTA on the European Economy: A Survey of Recent Empirics

Dr. Kuo-Chun Yeh

Associate Professor of Graduate Institute of National Development,

National Taiwan University

Abstract

This survey is mainly based on the empirics by the European Commission (2015) and Plasmans and Stavrevska (2014). As the first new generation free trade agreement, the progress of the EU-Korea FTA is of course an important reference to the rest East Asian economies to strengthen their links with the EU. After four-year implementation, it is clear that the FTA has worked well for both sides, in particular for the EU, according to the aggregate statistics and econometric research.

I. Introduction

Experiencing a series of asymmetric shocks (e.g., sovereign debt and refugee crises), EU badly needs an economic structural reform. If the EU authorities really care about the future of the euro, they should seriously carry out a long-term reform to eliminate economic asymmetry among the member states, instead of paying attention to the volumes of debt only. On the basis of the optimum currency area, an EU-level trade policy is an important part to achieve economic symmetry and sustainability, even if a political union will not be feasible in the near future. The EU-Korea FTA, the first of a new generation FTAs, has of course become a benchmark.

2016 marked the fifth anniversary of the EU-Korea FTA, which has been provisionally applied since July 2011. As the European Commission indicates (2016), it is the first of a new generation of FTAs and goes further than any previous agreements in lifting trade barriers. Besides, it is also the EU's first trade deal with an Asian country. Three important characteristics are as follows:

First, the agreement eliminates duties for industrial and agricultural goods in a progressive, step-by-step approach. The majority of import duties were removed already when the FTA entered into force on 1 July 2011. On 1 July 2016, import duties will be eliminated on all products except for a limited number of agricultural products;

Second, In addition to eliminating duties on nearly all trade in goods, the FTA addresses non-tariff barriers to trade with specific focus on the automotive, pharmaceuticals, medical devices and electronics sectors;

Finally, the agreement also creates new opportunities for market access in services and investments, and includes provisions in areas such as competition policy, government procurement, intellectual property rights, transparency in regulation and sustainable development.

Look at the recent statistics by Korean International Trade Association (2016), the EU exports to South Korea of goods decreased from 62.4 billion USD in 2014 to 57.2 billion USD in 2015. EU imports from South Korea decreased from 51.7 billion USD in 2014 to 48.1 billion USD in 2015. The main reason for the weaker performance of the imports from South Korea has been the decreased demand in the EU due to the economic downturn. However, in the third and fourth year of FTA implementation imports from South Korea increased annually by 5-6%. The European Commission (2015) believes that this gives a clear indication that the FTA has worked well also for South Korea. As a result, the EU's trade deficit with South Korea has turned into a trade surplus of 9.12 billion USD in 2015.

This report is to introduce the impact of the EU-Korea FTA on the European economy. Before that we can also see Korean perspectives (Garikipati 2015; Ministry of Trade, Industry and Energy in Korea 2014) about the FTA:

First, the EU's share in Korea's total imports from the world increased from 9 percent before the FTA to 11 percent in the third year of the FTA implementation. Over the same period of time, the EU's share in total exports from Korea declined from 11 percent to 9 percent;

Second, three sectors such as ships, automobiles and electronics represent almost 60 percent of Korea's total exports to the EU It means Korea's exports are not really much diversified after the launch of the FTA. As far as EU imports from Korea are concerned, the main product categories are "machinery and appliances" accounting for 36 percent of EU imports from Korea they have declined by 20 percent since the FTA took effect. "Transport equipment" accounting for 26 percent of total EU imports from Korea, showing fluctuating growth;

Thirdly, according to a recent survey of 360 major companies in 18

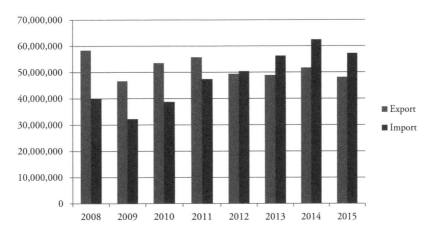

Figure 1: Korea's trade with the EU (Thousand USD)
Source: Korean International Trade Association (KITA 2016)

EU member countries, more than seven out of 10 European companies are taking advantage of the FTA to promote their business opportunities. The awareness of the Korea-EU FTA among European companies is far higher than that for the EU's free trade deals with other countries.

In sum, it is expected that the EU-Korea FTA should be a win-win game. The Korean government has its task cut out for it to ensure that the effects of the trade deal benefit both sides. However, at present it appears to be one-sided according to Korean evaluation. In this context, it is necessary to increase the utilization rate of the FTAs in the short run and to use the FTA as occasions to strengthen industrial competitiveness in the long run. Does European viewpoint is consistent with the above Korean evaluation?

II. Impact of the FTA on the EU

In addition to the annual report by the European Commission (2015), Plasmans and Stavrevska (2014) also use the gravity model, matching approach, and the difference-in-difference model to analyze the effect of the EU-Korea FTA on the EU.

The gravity equation in international trade has now been used for nearly 50 years to examine the effects on bilateral trade flows of various economic and/or political factors. In most instances, bilateral trade flows in a particular year are explained by relevant exporting country variables and importing country variables, such as exporter's and importer's gross domestic product (GDP) and indices of prices inclusive of exchange rates that vary over time, and also by time-invariant bilaterally fixed factors influencing trade costs, such as bilateral distance and dummy variables for shared languages or borders. These equations have considerable explanatory power.

The following is a typical gravity equation in equation where some variables specified below are in logarithms

$$y_{ij,t} = \varphi(\text{GDP}_{i,t}, \text{GDP}_{j,t}, \text{P}^X_{i,t}, \text{P}^M_{j,t}, \text{FTA}_{ij,t}, \text{Other}_{i,t}, \text{Other}_{j,t}, \text{Other}_{ij}, \varepsilon_{ij,t})$$

where $y_{ij,t}$ denotes the (logarithmic) real bilateral trade flow from (country) i to (country) j in period (quarter) t, where real denotes the nominal flow divided by the exporter's export price index, $\text{GDP}_{i,t}$ is the real gross domestic product of i in quarter t, $\text{GDP}_{j,t}$ is the real GDP of j in t, $\text{P}^X_{j,t}$ is a logarithmic index of export prices (including exchange rates) of i in t, $\text{P}^M_{j,t}$ a logarithmic index of import prices (including exchange rates), $\text{FTA}_{ij,t}$ is a dummy variable having a value of 1 from the date of inception of the corresponding bilateral FTA and 0 before, Other_{ij} denotes any time-invariant factor that naturally enhances or diminishes trade from i to j (such as their bilateral distance, a common land border, a common language, belonging to the same continent); $\text{Other}_{i,t}$ and $\text{Other}_{j,t}$ are other time-variant factors influencing exports of i and imports of j in quarter t, respectively, while $\varepsilon_{ij,t}$ is any unobserved random factor influencing the real bilateral trade flow $y_{ij,t}$ (this is also called the unobserved heterogeneity in fixed effects panel data models).

In Table 1 an overview of pooled (OLS-based) panel gravity model estimations is presented for the sample period 2000I –2013IV, where the variable is according to the EU-Korea FTA a dummy variable with a value of zero up to the second quarter of 2011 and a value of one for the sub-period 2011III-2013IV. It is important to note that the estimation is bilateral country pair specific and the trade flows are (one-way) gross real trade flows. Hence, we derive an estimate of the average effect of the EU-Korea FTA.

For the whole of exports from the EU27 to Korea this effect is most significant when we delete the index of export prices. We have to note that the price indices are from a different source (IFS) as the trade data (Eurostat). Excluding this price term the pooled estimate for the semi-elasticity of the EU-Korea FTA on the trade flow from the EU27 to Korea yields a very significant positive impact of 0.52 (0.42 for the product of the GDP variables).

The impact of the EU-Korea FTA dummy on the reverse trade flow is significantly negative but not very sizeable (point estimate of -0.02; -0.167 for the case with a product of the GDP variables). These observations are in correspondence with the rising effect of the EU-Korea FTA on the EU27 exports to Korea and the falling effect of this FTA implementation on the EU27 imports from Korea.

The impact of the distance dummy is in accordance with that of the FTA variable. It means the variable is very significantly positive on EU27 exports to Korea and significantly negative for EU imports from Korea.

Notice also the very significant positive impact of the multiple of trade partners' GDPs on both bilateral trade flows. Note that other models as matching and difference-in difference approaches show the similar empirical results.

III. Evaluation and Conclusion

According to the latest official evaluation by the European Commission (2015), the EU-Korea FTA has worked well for both sides, in particular for the EU. The weaker performance of Korean exports has to be seen in the context of the decreased demand in the EU following the financial crisis. However, the EU also stressed that the FTA has mitigated the impact of the crisis on Korean exports and that without the FTA, the Korean exports to the EU would have been hit much harder.

The official evaluation is also supported by academic research. A result that can be said to be common to the three methods (gravity model, matching, and difference-in difference) used is the existence of a clear-cut break since the inception of the EU-Korea FTA in July 2011. The pooled gravity model estimate for the semi-elasticity of the EU-Korea FTA on the trade flow from the EU27 to Korea yields a very significant positive impact of 0.52 (0.42 for the product of the GDP variables); the impact of the EU-Korea FTA dummy on the reverse trade flow is

Table 1: Empirics of the gravity model

Variable	Model1	Model2	Model3	Model4	Model5	Model6
Real EU-27 GDP	0.88** (0.01) [84.01]	0.94** (0.01) [56.78]		1.003** (0.0005) [1846.686]	1.01** (0.0017) [569.9]	
Real(S.) Korean GDP	-0.31 (0.32) [-0.95]	0.38** (0.22) [1.76]		0.04 (0.06) [0.68]	0.17** (0.04) [3.86]	
Mulitiple of trade partners GDPs			0.94** (0.01) [56.35]			1.006** (0.002) [500.44]
Distance	3.38** (0.11) [28.8]	3.36** (0.12) [27.79]	3.36** (0.12) [27.75]	-0.015** (0.003) [-5.09]	-0.04** (0.007) [-5.16]	-0.04** (0.007) [-4.96]
FTA dummy	0.13** (0.056) [2.3]	0.52** (0.062) [8.33]	0.42** (0.037) [11.24]	-0.093* (0.017) [-5.47]	-0.02** (0.009) [-2.15]	-0.167** (0.02) [-7.6]
EU average export prices	3.4** (0.26) [12.92]					
EU average import prices				0.6** (0.05) [11.88]		
Constant	-49.86** (7.72) [-6.45]	-54.38** (5.53) [-10.18]	-68.8** 1.36) [-50.75]	-17.55** (1.6) [_10.9]	-18.2** (1.14) [-15.9]	-39.78** (0.09) [-441.32]

Source: Plasmans and Stavrevska (2014)

Note: In the first three columns the dependent variable is the real EU27 export with IFS export deflator, while in the last three columns the dependent variable is real imports with IFS import deflator. The values of all variables, except for FTA, are in natural logarithms. Regressions are based on data for a single trade partner to the EU countries, namely, (South) Korea.

significantly negative but not very sizeable (point estimate of -0.02; -0.167 for the case with a product of the GDP variables). These findings are in correspondence with the rising effect of the EU-Korea FTA on the EU27 exports to Korea and the falling effect of this FTA implementation on the EU27 imports from Korea previously observed. The impact of the distance dummy is in accordance with that of the FTA variable: very significantly positive on EU27 exports to Korea and significantly negative for EU imports from Korea and the very significant positive impact of the multiple of trade partners' GDPs on both bilateral trade flows is also remarkable.

Reference

Council of the EU (2015). EU-South Korea free trade agreement concluded, 2015.10.1.

Garikipati, Ram (2015). Does Korea benefit from FTA with EU? The Korea Herald, http://www.koreaherald.com/view.php?ud=20150727001080, 2015.7.27.

European Commission (2016). Country and region: South Korea, http://ec.europa.eu/trade/policy/countries-and-regions/countries/south-korea/.

European Commission (2015). Annual report on the implementation of the EU-Korea free trade agreement, 2015.3.26.

Korean International Trade Association (2016). K-statistics, http://global.kita.net/kStat/byCountEcon_SpeCountBloc.do, 2016.4.11.

Ministry of Trade, Industry and Energy in Korea (2014). Analysis on the effect of Korea-EU FTA and successful cases on the anniversary of the Korea-EU FTA, 2014.7.1 (in Korean).

Plasmans, J. and V. Stavrevska (2014). Evaluating the impact of the EU-Korea Free Trade Agreement on the European Economy, working paper.

Prospective and Challenge of the Synergies between the Juncker Investment Plan and the Belt & Road

Prof. Dr. Li-Jiuan Chen-Rabich, LL.M

Professor of Graduate Institute of European Studies, Tamkang University

Jean Monnet Chair on European Trade Law

Dr. Jiann-Jong Guo

Associate Professor of Graduate Institute of China Studies, Tamkang University

I. Introduction

The European Fund for Strategic Investments (EFSI), a key component of Juncker's investment plan, was adopted in June 2015. It is expected to raise €315bn for the real economy in EU. The EFSI will provide funding for not just long-term infrastructure investments but also for the SME and mid-cap enterprises.[1] In the first phase, the fund will run four years. The EU will provide a capital guarantee of €16bn and the European Investment Bank (EIB) €5bn. By leveraging up and the participation of other investors, the fund aims to gather €315bn in investments and create up to 1.3 million new jobs.[2]

The "Belt and Road" initiative, proposed by the Chinese President Xi Jinping in 2013, was widely viewed as a major strategic move for China for its economic development and its global economic role. The "Belt and Road" seeks to link China with Europe through central and

---

[1] Industrial Policy Dossier, Juncker's Investment Plan for Europe. Opportunities for German Companies, Bundesverband der Deutschen Industrie e.V. 23/07/2015, p.1.

[2] Ibid. p.1.

western Asia via the New Silk Road Economic Belt and connect China with Southeast Asian countries, Africa and Europe through the 21st Century Maritime Silk Road.[3]

In the seventeenth China-EU summit in June 2015, EU and China both declared to build synergies between the Jean-Claude Juncker's investment plan and the "Belt and Road". Three months later during a high-level economic dialogue, Brussels announced that China became the first non-EU country to announce contribution to the Juncker Plan.[4] This short article is trying to find out the prospective and challenge of the synergies between them.

II Objectives of Juncker's investment plan and the "Belt and Road"

1. *The objectives of Juncker's investment plan*

The objective of the Juncker's investment package is to increase competitiveness and stimulate economic growth for EU countries. As investments in Europe have been declining for the last decade, and the growth potential on the continent has increased at a slower pace compared with some of its trading partners. The backlog of private and public investments has been caused by a lack of liquidity and

---

[3] The first route, the New Silk Road Economic Belt, will run westward overland through Central Asia and onward to Europe. The second route, the 21st-Century Maritime Silk Road, will probably loop south and westward by sea towards Europe, with proposed stops in South-east Asia, South Asia and Africa. The Economist, 2015, Prospects and Challenges on China's one belt, one road: a risk assessment report, from the Economist Intelligence Unit, www.eiu.com, p.3. Xinhua, February 18, 2016, China focus on Belt & Road, Juncker plan synergies http://www.chinadailyasia.com/nation/2016-02/18/content_15386616.html.

[4] So far, no precise amount of investment figure has been announced by both sides.

by other non-financial barriers as well.[5] Before introduction of the Juncker's investment plan, the EU's environment faced several barriers for investment. Most troublesome barriers include: 1. lack of investor confidence; 2. Stretch too much in public budgets; 3. credit crunch in crisis-hit countries; 4. obstructive financial market regulations; 5. lack of venture capital; 6. uncertainty and volatility scare off investors; 7. state investments have dropped significantly since 2009; 8. despite low interest rates, companies are not getting loans because of their risk profiles and general uncertainty; 9. compliance and risk regulations make corporate financing uninteresting or impossible for investors;10. start-ups and young companies have particular difficulties acquiring capital.[6]

According to a report, the actual EU's investment level is currently 15% lower than its peak in 2007.[7] Such inadequate levels of investment over past decade have caused many European companies to become less competitive. This is a particular problem for the high-tech industry, which is suffering badly from the stagnation in R&D activities. EU R&D intensity, at just over 2%, is currently well short of countries like Japan and South Korea, who have already exceeded 3% and gradually increasing their competitiveness. A similar picture exists with patent applications, where the EU is again lagging behind. Europe is in danger of losing its ability to keep up in the global innovation race.[8] According to the European Investment Bank, annual sums of €435bn are needed to fill the investment gaps in Europe selected sectors (please see table 1).

[5] Industrial Policy Dossier, Juncker's Investment Plan for Europe. Opportunities for German Companies, Bundesverband der Deutschen Industrie e.V. 23/07/2015, p.1.

[6] Ibid. p.4.

[7] Ibid. p.4 .

[8] Ibid. p.5.

Table1: Annual investment required by selected sectors in the EU Area

	Investment volumes needed (in billion euros)
Research & Development	130
Energy grids	100
Transport networks	50
Digitalisation of the economy	55
Educational facilities	10
Environment, water, climate	90
total	435 billion euros

Source: EIB 2015a[9]

2. Objectives of the "Belt and Road" Policy

The political and economic objectives of the "Belt and Road" are firstly to solve the Chinese problem of industrial overcapacity; secondly to access natural resources from abroad and finally to strengthen its national security by connecting some developing countries in Asian, African and European regions.

(1)   Solving the problem of industrial overcapacity and inventory

According to IMF estimates, the general normal industrial capacity utilization should be more than 85%, while the Chinese industrial capacity utilization does not exceed 70%. In the end of 2012, the capacity utilization of Chinese iron and steel, cement, electrolytic aluminum, flat glass and vessel industry was only of 72%, 73.7%, 71.9%, 73.1% and 75% respectively, significantly lower than the international general standard.[10] By 2013, either the high-energy-intensive sectors such as aluminum, iron and steel manufacturing, or solar and wind power of newly emerging industries, as well as the high-end products

---

[9]   Ibid. p.6.

[10]   General Office of the State Council of P.R.C.,"The guidance of the State Council to resolve serious contradiction in excess capacity of supply, Guo Fa [2013] No. 41, October 15, 2013.

such as silicon steel of shipbuilding and steel industries are also in overcapacity. The policy of OBOR helped to explore new market in those developing countries along the OBOR routes which is expected to absorb the Chinese industrial inventory to some degree to ease the Chinese industrial overcapacity.[11]

(2)   Accessing Oil, gas and mineral resources from abroad

Chinese Oil and gas resources are highly dependent on import from foreign countries. According to the Chinese Academy of Social Sciences, the "China World Energy Outlook (2013-2014)" reports that the Chinese overall dependence on foreign energy sources increased from 9% in 2013 to 11% in 2015, and will be nearly 26% in 2020. Taking Oil and natural gas as an example, China's dependence on foreign oil was around 55% in 2011, it went up to 60% by 2015. Dependence on foreign natural gas increased from around 19% in 2013 to 35% in 2015, it will close to 40% in 2020. While more than 80% natural gas were imported from Australia.

In addition to oil, natural gas, China also imported substantial iron ore, copper ore, bauxite, coal and other resources, but the main channel for importing them is through the sea, the risk is high. The OBOR can add a large number of resources imported from developing countries along the OBOR routes by land channels, which increased the safety for transportation.[12]

(3)   Strengthen Chinese national security

Most developed industrial and infrastructure facilities in China are concentrated in coastal areas, oil, gas, and mineral resources, largely import through the coast into Chinese mainland, so the Chinese government is afraid of any threat from the sea which may hit its

---

[11] Guo Jiann-jong, 2015, China "One Belt One Road" Strategies Changing the Relations with Developing Countries, Studies on Chinese Communism, vol.49, no.3, pp. 42-59.
[12] Ibid. pp. 42-59.

economy badly. So Beijing hopes through the design of OBOR to increase the development of its central and western regions in order to deploy some of key industrial sectors in those regions. Especially in the western regions, sparsely populated and less industry, there is a great industrial and infrastructure development potential, and less threats in wartime, therefore to integrate this part of China into the countries along the Silk Road Economic Belt routes would   bring benefits to its own national security.[13]

III Financial Cooperation of Juncker's investment and the "Belt and Road"

1   Financial plan of Juncker's investment

The Juncker's investment plan was first presented at 26 November 2014, and the regulation establishing the European Fund for Strategic Investments (EFSI) was approved by the European Parliament and the Council in June 2015. The EFSI, which is the heart of the investment plan, can now become operational.[14] The EFSI is set to mobilise €315bn. The EFSI will be financed with €21bn: €5bn from the European Investment Bank (EIB), and €16bn from the EU. €21bn will be expanded to €315bn by applying 15 leverage ratio which will come from the additional capital raised by the EIB and from the participation of private investors (such as pension funds, insurance companies, etc.). Among them, €240bn will go to larger investment projects, and €75bn to SMEs and mid-caps.[15]

---

[13] Ibid. pp. 42-59.

[14] Industrial Policy Dossier, Juncker's Investment Plan for Europe. Opportunities for German Companies, Bundesverband der Deutschen Industrie e.V. 23/07/2015, p.7.

[15] Ibid. p.7.

This fund is running by a steering board, a managing director and an investment committee. The committee will be responsible for approving the support of the EU guarantee to the EIB for certain investment projects. The EIB will handle the processing. Financing for investments by SMEs and mid-caps will primarily come from the European Investment Fund (EIF). In order to support the implementation of investment projects, two other instruments will be set up independently of the EFSI: an investment portal (EIPP) that will present projects to interested investors, and a hub for investment advice (EIAH) that will serve as the central point of contact for technical support and advisory services. The EFSI is to be accompanied by a package of measures designed to remove barriers from investment. For example, the Capital Markets Union and structural reforms should improve the overall investment climate.[16]

2. *Financial plan of the "Belt and Road"*

Moreover, China has created the financial platform and vehicles for the "Belt and Road" projects, such as the establishment of the AIIB ($100bn), the New Silk Road Fund (NSRF, $40bn), the China-CEE Fund (Central and Eastern Europe, $435mln)[17] and numerous bilateral pledges. With the BRICS's New Development Bank also in operational, there will be plenty of funding sources to expedite developmental projects in the countries along the OBOR routes.[18]

---

[16] Ibid. p.7.

[17] CEE Equity Partners Ltd is the investment advisor for the China-CEE Fund with committed funds of $435 mln. The Fund was established by China Exim Bank in partnership with other institutional investors from the CEE region to capitalize on investment opportunities in CEE countries. The objective of the Fund is to identify and partner with dynamic businesses and together contribute to the vibrant growth of the CEE economies whilst providing good returns to the investors.

[18] Dragan Pavlićević, 15July 31, 2015, China, the EU and One Belt, One Road Strategy, Publication: China Brief Volume: 15 Issue. http://www.jamestown.org/programs/

Moreover, The Chinese government also offered budgets for its state-owned enterprises to invest in the countries along the OBOR routes. For example, in 2015, the Chinese outward foreign direct investment (OFDI) to 49 countries along the OBOR routes reached $14.82bn.[19] This type of Chinese internal budgets is more flexible than other source of funds for the projects related to the OBOR.

3. Financial Cooperation between "Juncker's investment" and "Belt and Road"

The matter of negotiating financial cooperation between the Juncker's investment plan and the OBOR was taking place in the 17th China-EU summit at 29 June, 2015, in Brussels. In his keynote speech for this summit, Li Keqiang said: "China will actively consider establishing a China-EU joint investment fund to support the EFSI. China will increase the purchase of EIB bonds. We may fully tap pan-European investment cooperation platform, China CEEC[20] framework for investment and financing, AIIB and other financial arrangements, and expand cooperation with Europe through the Silk Road Fund...to ensure that financial cooperation become a bond that link our common interests."[21] The EU Commission President Jean Claude Juncker responded to Li's statement is that, "If we can make it work-and I hope we can- I see huge benefits for both China and the EU."[22]

---

chinabrief/single/?tx_ttnews%5Btt_news%5D=44235&cHash=9 dbc08472c19ecd69130 7c4c1905eb0c#.VvErWeJ96Uk.

[19] People's Republic of China central government website, http://www.gov.cn, 03/05/2016.

[20] China-Central and Eastern European Countries (CEEC).

[21] Keynote Speech by Li Keqiang, 29 June 2015, China and Europe: Working Together for New Progress In China-EU Relations, At China-EU Business Summit, http://www.fmprc.gov.cn/mfa_eng/zxxx_662805/t1277193.shtml

[22] https://euobserver.com/eu-china/129318.

It is reported that China could invest up to €10bn in the EU's new infrastructure fund; but a final decision is being held up by the complex mechanics of a deal to give Chinese technology companies a greater role in Europe.[23]

IV The Mechanisms for Both Sides to Promote Economic Cooperation and Executions

In order to promote substantive cooperation between the Juncker investment plan and the "One Belt One Road", the Chinese government and the European Union, under the "comprehensive strategic partnership", established some types of mechanism for cooperation and dialogue. They are: (1) top leader's meeting mechanism; (2) high-level official strategic dialogue; (3) high-level economic and trade dialogue; (4) senior level of humanitarian and cultural exchange and dialogue mechanism, a so-called three pillars of the "1 + 3" high-level dialogue pattern. In these mechanisms, the top leader's meeting mechanism is the highest official level of meeting mechanism. Any consensus reached during the end of meeting and dialogue within these four types of mechanism, or cooperation projects signed, will have a joint statement issued or a joint press released.[24] Between 2013 and 2015, ten more crucial contracts and agreements have been signed between China and countries in the EU. (Please see table 2)

---

[23] http://www.euractive.com/sections/innovation-industry/chinas-bid-eu-investment-fund-trips-complex- rules-316244

[24] Xinhua networking, http://news.xinhuanet.com/ziliao/2004-05/08/content_1457067. htm.

Table 2: Ten crucial contracts and agreements signed between China and EU countries

1. China and EU and key Countries		
Year	**Partner**	**Contracts or Agreements**
Dec.21, 2013	China and EU	*China-EU 2020 Strategic Agenda for Cooperation*
Mar.31, 2014	China and EU	*The Joint Statement on Deepening Mutually Beneficial and Win-Win China-EU Comprehensive Strategic Partnership*
June, 2015	China and EU	*Joint Declaration and the Joint Statement on Climate Change*
Oct.10, 2014	China and Germany	*Sino-German Cooperation Platform for Action: A Total Mutual Innovation*
Oct.22, 2015	China and UK	*Sino-British Joint Declaration on the Construction of the 21st century global comprehensive strategic partnership*
2. Economic cooperation between China and Central and Eastern European countries		
Nov.26, 2013	China and Central & Eastern Europe	*The Bucharest Guidelines for Cooperation between China and Central and Eastern European Countries*
Dec.17, 2014	China and Central & Eastern Europe	*The Belgrade Guidelines for Cooperation between China and Central and Eastern European Countries*
Nov.25, 2015	China and Central & Eastern Europe	*The Medium-Term Agenda for Cooperation between China and Central and Eastern European Countries*
Nov.25, 2015	China and Central & Eastern Europe	*The Suzhou Guidelines for Cooperation between China and Central and Eastern European Countries*
June, 2015	China and Hungary	The two governments signed a memorandum of understanding to jointly promote "One Belt One Road" construction, Hungary became the first European country to sign on the documents of "One Belt One Road" with China.

V Industrial synergies of the Juncker's investment plan and the Belt & Road

1. Current development

So far up to now, cooperation between these two projects have made some progress on, particularly in prioritized areas including connectivity, financing and digital economy.[25] In January 2016, the first working group meeting of China-EU connectivity Platform was convened as a follow-up to the MOU on the establishment of EU-China connectivity platform.

In terms of connectivity, they agreed to share information, promote seamless traffic flows and transport facilitation, develop synergies between relevant initiatives and projects, identify cooperation opportunities between respective policies and sources of funding. The two sides will work to "actively explore business and investment opportunities" and create a favorable environment for sustainable and inter-operable cross-border infrastructure networks in countries and regions between China and the EU, said Yang Yanyi, head of Chinese Mission to the EU.[26]

On financing issue, the two sides have so far held three meetings of technical working group on China-EU Cooperation on Investment. During the latest one in January this year (2016), experts from China's Silk Road Fund, the European Commission, and the European Investment Bank exchanged views on co-investment vehicle."Both sides are committed to developing concrete opportunities for China to invest in the Juncker's investment plan for Europe," the ambassador Yang Yanyi said.[27]

---

[25] Xinhua, February 18, 2016, China focus on Belt & Road, Juncker plan synergies http://www.chinadailyasia.com/nation/2016-02/18/content_15386616.html.

[26] Ibid.

[27] Ibid.

2. Infrastructure perspective

With infrastructure as a part of great significance in both the Juncker investment Plan and "One Belt One Road" initiative, Brussels and Beijing agreed to further improve their infrastructure links in the following three industrial fields.[28]

(1) The first industrial field for cooperation: transport infrastructure projects

The Juncker investment plan and the OBOR both regard the transport infrastructure projects as a priority area for docking. Juncker investment plan can docking along with the OBOR in transport infrastructure projects, including: the Trans-European Transport Network (TEN-T)[29], the Central Europe Land-Sea Express and the new Eurasian Continental Bridge. Taking the TEN-T Connecting Europe as an example, this plan seeks to connect existing roads, railways, airports and canals and other transportation infrastructure together, in order to achieve a completion of the unified transportation system in Europe by 2030. Currently this project is co-financed by the European Unicom facility (CEF) and the European Investment Bank (EIB). After the EFSI established, then about 30% of this funds are expected to invest in the field of transport infrastructure.[30] But it is still not enough financially.

China active in promoting transport infrastructure projects docking with Europe, mainly because of its well developed railway industry possessed two high-speed rail technologies: the locomotive technology

---

[28] Ibid.

[29] Mobility and Transport , European Commission, http://ec.europa.eu/transport/infrastructure/tentec/tentec-portal/site/en/abouttent.htm

[30] Li Gang,2016, China Academy of Social Science, Institute of European Studies, How China "One Belt One Road" to dock European "Juncker plan"?, "China Economic Weekly" (2016, No. 3), http://paper.people.com.cn/zgjjzk/html/2016-01/18/content_1649509.htm. Zh Shuai, Saidi think tank, 2016, How to achieve "One Belt One Road" dock with "Juncker plan", http://www.ccidgroup.com/sdgc/7072.htm.

and the rail technology. Moreover, May 2015, the Chinese State Department issued the "guidance on the promotion of international production and equipment manufacturing cooperation" in the hope to give full play of its high speed train advantages in the infrastructure field, in order to actively promote the Chinese steel, construction machinery and other industries to "go out".

Actually, before trying to promote a synergize of the Juncker investment plan and the OBOR, Chinese companies have already actively explored the infrastructure market in Eastern European countries and receiving a number of bridges, power plants, highways and other construction projects. Among them, the first use of China's preferred embodiment loan to build a bridge across the Danube river in Belgrade of Serbia was opened to traffic in 2014. At the same time, Serbia E763 motorway and Macedonia two highways are also in the process of construction.[31] E763 motorway is the first project put into practice under the China - Central and Eastern Europe cooperation framework for cooperation in the field of infrastructure.

The most typical case in terms of the cooperation in transportation infrastructure between the Juncker investment plan and the OBOR is the Hungarian - Serbia railway project. "The project is said to be the first concrete success of the China-Central and Eastern European Countries (CEEC) partnership."[32]

According a news report, two documents for a high-speed railway linking Serbia and Hungary were signed on Nov. 24 (2015) showing

[31] People's Republic of China central government website, Xinhua News Agency, http://big5.gov.cn/gate/big5/www.gov.cn/xinwen/2015-11/23/content_5015786.htm. Financial Observer: "along the way" to lead China - Central and Eastern Europe economic and trade cooperation, November 23, 2015, http://www.get-top-news.com/news-11036747.html.

[32] China wins $1.6bn contract to support Hungary-Serbia high-speed rail, 26 November 2015 ,http://www.railway-technology.com/news/newschina-wins-16bn-contract-to-support-hungary-serbia-high-speed-rail-4738236.

China's continuing efforts to boost ties with the Central and Eastern European countries.

In a ceremony witnessed by Premier Li Keqiang and Hungarian Prime Minister Viktor Orban, China's National Development and Reform Commission and Hungary's Foreign Affairs and Trade Ministry signed an agreement to cooperate on the development, construction and financing of the Hungarian section of the Hungary-Serbia railway. Additionally, China Railway International and China Communications Construction Co. have signed a contract with the Serbian Ministry of Mining and Energy for the modernization and reconstruction of the Serbian section of the railway.[33] Actually, before the agreement signed by three parties, in June 2015, during the Chinese Minister of Foreign Affairs Wang Yi visit to Hungary, the "Hungary-Serbia" railway construction project has already been incorporated into the "OBOR" cooperation framework.

Under the agreement, a consortium led by China Railway Group (CRG) has been awarded a CNY10bn ($1.57bn) contract to build the 160km Hungarian section of a railway linking Budapest with Belgrade, and will also be responsible for the general management of the project. In addition to CRG, the consortium includes CRG's China Railway International Group (CRIG), China Railway International (CRI), a subsidiary of national operator of China Railway Corporation and Hungarian State Railways. Both CRI and CRIG will jointly hold an 85% stake in the consortium. The Chinese firms will finance 85% of the project, while the remaining 15% will come from Hungary.[34]

Construction of the Hungary-Serbia railway began in 2015; the train link, which will cut travel time between Belgrade and Budapest

---

[33] People's Republic of China central government website, Xinhua News Agency, http://www.gov.cn/xinwen/2015-11/26/content_5017234.htm.

[34] China Daily, Nov 25, 2015, High-speed railway set for Hungary, Serbia, http://english.gov.cn/premier/news/2015/11/25/content_281475241762006.htm.

from eight hours to three, will be finished in two years (in 2017).[35]

(2) The second industrial field for cooperation: the electrical energy projects

In order to reduce the EU's dependence on oil and natural gas energy, EU, in February 2015, announced a strategic framework of energy alliance within Europe, one of the important project in that strategic framework is to achieve a 10% grid interconnection by 2020. According to a projection made by EU at the end of 2014, the EU construction of cross-border energy network in the energy sector need to invest €200bn by 2020. Therefore, after the establishment of EFSI, around 30% of the EFSI funds is expected to invest in the energy field. Therefore, one of the important initiatives along the synergies between these OBOR and the Juncker investment plan is to docking in the field of electrical energy, which will bring new market opportunities for both companies in the construction of power grids and transmission equipment manufacturing.[36]

In practice, while both sides are trying to arranging synergies for the two grand projects, China has execute several cooperative projects with the Central and Eastern European countries already. For example, the first to use China - Central and Eastern European Cooperation Mechanism $10bn special credit line for thermal power station projects in Bosnia and Herzegovina Steiner have been starting construction. In addition, the loan agreement for the Serbian branch Stolac Plant Phase II project has been signed;the Gezhouba major thermal power company (葛

---

[35] Premier Li told an economic and trade forum during the Fourth Summit of China and Central and Eastern European Countries (16+1), which was held in Suzhou on Nov 24, 2015.

[36] Li Gang,2016, China Academy of Social Science, Institute of European Studies, How China "One Belt One Road" to dock European "Juncker plan"?, "China Economic Weekly" (2016, No. 3) , http://paper.people.com.cn/zgjjzk/html/2016-01/18/content_1649509.htm.

洲壩公司) won the bid of constructing the Tuzla thermal power station through an international tender; the Huadian Group (華電集團) won the Romania Weiner fired power plant project; in November 9 of 2015, the China Guangdong Nuclear Power Group (CGNPC, 中國廣核集團), which been selected as the sole investor by the relevant authorities in Romania, with the Romania government signed the memorandum of development and construction and operation of the Cernavoda Nuclear Power Station Unit 3 and 4 project.[37]

(3) The third industrial field for Cooperation: the internet & communications infrastructure networking

On digital economy, the two sides sought to achieve a better synergy between Europe's digital agenda and China's Internet Plus strategy and to benefit the 1.1 billion internet users in both China and the EU. They signed a key partnership on 5G telecommunications in September (2015) and now, according to Yang, were taking steps to deepen dialogues and cooperation in areas of information and communications technology.[38]

Actually, in the field of the digital economy, the Chinese optical fiber & cable communications equipment manufacturers are in the most mature condition to cooperate with the "Juncker investment plan". On the one hand, the current investment in the network infrastructure by European telecom enterprises is at a slower rate than other countries, while the internet communication infrastructure is an important supporter to the European telecommunication's economy. According to a report released by the Independent Authority of CRU MARKET

---

[37] People's Republic of China central government website, Xinhua News Agency, http://big5.gov.cn/gate/big5/www.gov.cn/xinwen/2015-11/23/content_5015786.htm. Financial Observer: "along the way" to lead China - Central and Eastern Europe economic and trade cooperation, November 23, 2015, http://www.get-top-news.com/news-11036747.html.

[38] Xinhua, February 18, 2016, China focus on Belt & Road, Juncker plan synergies http://www.chinadailyasia.com/nation/2016-02/18/content_15386616.html.

ANALYSIS in 2014, the demand growth of cable in Western Europe reached 20%, especially the most significant growth took place in France and Italy, compared with 13% in Eastern Europe.

March 2015, the EU officially announced 5G public-private partnership vision program, and trying to achieve 5G network operator in 2020—2025 period. In fact as early as 2012, the European Union has launched the world's first large-scale international research projects of 5G METIS, and plans to launch 5G by 2020. After the EFSI been established, more capital (around 20% of the EFSI) are expected to be invested in the field of communications network,[39] this will increase the demand of optical fiber & cable of communication's infrastructural equipments. China is one of the country can benefit from that. Mainly because the Chinese optical fiber and cable communication equipment manufacturers, from materials to manufacturing technology and key equipment, has already formed an industrial chain. That's why China is very keen to offer cooperation with EU in the area of internet & communication infrastructure networking.

VI Conclusion: Constraints and Challenges for the synergies of these Two Plans

Although EU and China have actively try to create synergies for the Juncker investment plan and OBOR, they still face some constraints and challenges relating to the synergies of these two plans.

---

[39] Li Gang,2016, China Academy of Social Science, Institute of European Studies, How China "One Belt One Road" to dock European "Juncker plan"?, "China Economic Weekly" (2016, No. 3), http://paper.people.com.cn/zgjjzk/html/2016-01/18/content_1649509.htm. Zhu Shuai, Saidi think tank, 2016, How to achieve "One Belt One Road" dock with "Juncker plan", http://www.ccidgroup.com/sdgc/7072.htm.

1. *Financial Constrains of the Belt & Road*

In fact, the infrastructure development in many low-income countries along the OBOR routes still lags behind its economic growth, and in terms of quality or quantity of economic development are lower than international standards. Only within the Asian region, there is a huge funding gap. According to a prediction by the Asian Development Bank that in the next 10 years, Asian infrastructure investment needs $8.22 trillion, the annual demand for infrastructure funding will be $ 820bn.[40] Which is far more than the AIIB, the New Silk Road Fund, the China-CEE Fund and the BRICS's New Development Bank together can offer annually.

2. *Financial doubt on Juncker investment plan*

Since the Juncker investment plan been proposed, it started to under questioned and challenge financially. Doubts and critics concerned on two issues: First, according to the European Investment Bank's estimate, at least annual sum of €435bn are needed to fill the investment gaps in Europe selected sectors. But the total amount of Juncker investment plan is only about €315bn in 4 years, drop in the bucket, and caused doubts from many European companies and experts.

Second, some more serious questions are about: Can the €21bn be arranged smoothly? Can €21bn be increased up to €315bn by applying 15 leverage ratio, which is planning to attract the additional funds from private investors? According to a press reported, "Juncker's €315bn investment plan for EU is in trouble as Nobel scientists criticized a

---

[40] Experts say Asian investment bank should promote PPP: insufficient investment in infrastructure along the way funds, 2015,
http://www.like-news.us/?i722930-Experts-say-Asian-investment-bank-should-promote-PPP:-insufficient-investment-in-infrastructure-along-the-way-funds.

raid on space and research budget".[41] The new controversy revolves on the initial €21bn starting fund, which comprises €16bn from the Commission – €8bn in cash and a further €8bn in guarantees – and €5bn from the European Investment Bank. However, the €8bn Commission cash is not actually new money but merely transfers from other key budgets, e.g. €2.7bn is from the EU's pioneering research, space and innovation budget, which angered some Nobel prize winning scientists.[42]

The Chinese side has taken note on the financial constraints of Juncker investment plan. According to Liu Zuokui, the director of Central and Eastern Europe Research Division of CASS Institute of European Studies, pointed out that Juncker investment plan set up €21bn for start-up capital and trying to pry about 15 times leverage funds to reach up €315bn might not be feasible. He said: "leverage magnified so much, can it be successfully to bring together such huge funds is a big problem."[43]

3. Risk Assessments on OBOR

Given the wide range of countries and the sums of money involved in the OBOR plan, financial institutions will need to be cognizant of the range of credit risks present in OBOR countries. The Economist Intelligence Unit Limited (2015) provided a report of risk assessment, overall scores include risks across ten different categories, including security, legal and regulatory, government effectiveness, political instability and

---

[41] Nick Mathiason, February 16, 2015, Juncker's €315bn investment plan for EU in trouble as Nobel scientists criticise raid on space and research budget, https://www.thebureauinvestigates.com/2015/02/16/juncker-plan-315bn-investment-eu-trouble-nobel-scientists-criticise/.

[42] Ibid.

[43] Liu Zuokui, 2015, the director of Central and Eastern Europe Research Division of CASS Institute of European Studies,"one belt, one road"dock along with the Juncker investment plan, China Net, 2015-06-29, http://opinion.china.com.cn/opinion_4_132504.html.

infrastructure.[44]

According to the EIU, some developing countries along with the OBOR routers have face infrastructure risk. Especially, in the Association of Southeast Asian Nations (ASEAN), 7 countries' scores of infrastructure risk are higher than 50%: Myanmar (91%), Laos (78%), Cambodia (72%), the Philippines (59%), Indonesia (59%), Vietnam (56%) and Thailand (53%).[45] In terms of country credit risk, many the Middle East and Africa's countries scored high index, for example: Syria (85%), Sudan (83%), Yemen (75%), Libya (68%), Iraq and Iran (66%), Lebanon and Ethiopia (61%), Egypt (60%), Kenya (59%), Jordan (57%), Tunisia (56%) Uganda (55%), Tanzania (54%), Algeria (51%) and Morocco and Turkey (50%).[46]

Besides, political risks may weigh heavy on the execution of OBOR plan. Many OBOR projects are slated to be high-profile construction projects, which means that the deals will be made with the deep involvement of the destination country's government. Therefore, political changes need to be anticipated, as they can change the outcome of a deal.[47] Certainly, It has significant meaning to watch and to study how the OBOR plan is going to overcome those risks.

4. Factors affected Trust between the Juncker Investment Plan and the BOR

China-EU relations still has some problem, the two sides have some differences in the perceptions and ideas of each other. So far, EU has not

---

[44] The Economist, 2015, Prospects and Challenges on China's one belt, one road: a risk assessment report, from the Economist Intelligence Unit, www.eiu.com, pp.1-7.

[45] The Economist, 2015, Prospects and Challenges on China's one belt, one road: a risk assessment report, from the Economist Intelligence Unit, www.eiu.com, p.8.

[46] The Economist, 2015, Prospects and Challenges on China's one belt, one road: a risk assessment report, from the Economist Intelligence Unit, www.eiu.com, p.9.

[47] Ibid.

recognize China's market economy status;EU still prohibits arms exports to China, both issues has plagued China. Every time these two issues will be included in EU-China meeting. Moreover, EU still concerns about the Chinese human rights, religion and the rule of law, its enthusiasm never diminished, the annual EU-China human rights dialogue is one of an important part of the EU's foreign policy. Besides, some Europeans have the "fear of Chinese money". At a Brussels' workshop in June 2015, an Austrian said, " It's quite sensitive to speak about Chinese money coming into the region. We don't want to need money which does not come from Europe, or not from Austria, or not from the region."[48]

However, the above differences would not be disappeared due to the cooperation between the Juncker's plan and OBOR, but they are not serious enough to damage two sides' decision to promote economic coopcration. So far, it is still too early to evaluate the performance of economic synergies of the Juncker investment plan and OBOR, but it is quite important to keep closely watching the cooperative progress of these two grand projects, one from Asia and one from EU, and see what impacts they might have on the global political economy.

---

[48] http://euobserver.com/eu-china/128971.

The Transformation of EU's Global Trade Policies through the Transatlantic Trade and Investment Partnership

Reinhard Biedermann

Assistant Professor of Department of Global Politics and Economics,
Tamkang University

Abstract

The Transatlantic Trade and Investment Partnership (TTIP) negotiations between the European Union (EU) and the United States signify a recent twofold transformation of EU's global trade policy strategy. The first transformation are the negotiations as such, since they had been regarded as improbable only a decade ago. The second transformation of EU's strategy comes along with the negotiations. This essay wants to explore the reasons for these twofold transformations to better understand the causes and potential consequences for the EU's contribution to global standard setting, for which TTIP aims for. This paper first conducts a brief literature review on the EU-as-global-regulatory-actor debate that began in the 2000s with regard to the TTIP negotiations. Secondly, it will differentiate between normative, defensive and offensive neoliberal trade policy goals the EU and the USA pursue. Thirdly, it will analyse the general transformations of EU's trade policy with regard to the setting of future global trade standards.

I. Introduction

Since 2013 the European Union (EU) and the United States (USA) negotiate on a Transatlantic Trade and Investment Agreement (TTIP) to establish the world's largest free trade area. The agreement would comprise more than fourty percent of the world's economy and one third of the global trade flow. Hitherto, neither the EU nor the USA has shown a considerable interest to negotiate on a bilateral trade accord since the launch of the World Trade Organization (WTO) in 1995. On the contrary, both blanketed the world with free trade agreements with third actors to promote their own favoured policies and standards. Therefore, the negotiations on a transatlantic trade deal mark a paradigm shift, at least for the EU, since a bilateral trade deal may also question EU's often presumed leading role on setting global regulatory standards on products.

Both sides have a long wish list. The last remaining tariff barriers between them shall be abolished, which is a main goal by the European car industries. In terms of free trade, the EU is more open and liberal than the USA. Therefore, in exchange for lowering tariffs, the USA wants the EU to lower consumer standards. The USA wants to export genetically modified food, hormone-treated beef, and chlorine-washed chicken to the EU, which alerts European consumers. The USA wants to eradicate the EU's signature brand on consumer protection, the precautionary principle, while the EU wants open the protected US public procurement sector. The EU wants to use its new competence on negotiating Bilateral Investment Treaties (BIT) based on the model of the International Centre for Settlement of Investment Disputes (ICSID), while the USA prefers private arbitration. For the EU, procurement and investment rules play a huge role in global trade of the 21st century. Therefore, a common EU-USA approach could help set global standards during an era when the EU also negotiates on investment rules with China and on procurement with Southeast Asian states, where China's clout is getting stronger. To put it in a nutshell: would the EU give up its signature brand "precautionary principle" of consumer protection to make its large suppliers and multinational corporations more competitive on the Asian market?

In November 2015 the EU Commission published a new trade strategy, titled "Trade for All. Towards a more responsible trade and investment policy".[1] This new strategy is EU's answer particularly to civil society protests in European capitals against the TTIP negotiations. But it is also a result of US-EU negotiations on content. At time of writing (April 2016), it is far from sure that negotiations will be concluded successfully. In recent months on both sides of the transatlantic ocean a growing majority of people reject the plans on a free trade agreement. People fear that high EU standards are traded away for the sake of small elite of multinational corporations. Notwithstanding its potential failure, the negotiations already have a considerable impact on future trade agreements and the EU's role as a global regulatory standards setter.

The next section conducts a review on the EU-as-global-regulatory-actor debate that began roundabout in the middle of the last decade. It will explore when and how the EU projects power in trade relations, leaning on the most recent literature on that topic. Then, it will take a look on EU's trade policy priorities in comparison with the USA with regard to global projections of standards, structured along normative, neoliberal, and strategic goals. In discussing the transatlantic trade negotiations, this paper moderately tries to assess the future direction of EU's global standard setting capacities. I argue that the TTIP negotiations aim at defending the neoliberal policies of the past decades of globalization, but also emphasize normative policies like social and environmental standards. For both the USA and the EU, TTIP would

---

[1] European Commission, *Trade for all*. Towards a more responsible trade and investment strategy, accessed April 16, 2016, http://trade.ec.europa.eu/doclib/docs/2015/october/ tradoc_153846.pdf

be a chance to protect open markets, fair competition and human rights. However, the EU may have to pay the price for not being in a position anymore to promote its own "golden standards', since the lower US standards could gain the upper hand at global level.

II. The EU as a global regulatory actor and TTIP

It is widely accepted to portray the EU as a 'power' in the multilateral trading system. The EU with its 500 Million people still remains the largest trading actor in the world. She also ranks first in both inbound and outbound international investments. Economically the EU is a giant in the middle of a Euro-sphere of some 80 states, for whom the EU is the largest trading partner.[2] The EU's experience of market integration underpins also its external trade policy. The EU imports more from developing countries than the USA, Japan and China together (fuels excluded). Since they depend on trade with and investment from the centre, public regulators in trade partner countries have to be trained on European standards and implement them if they want to enable their corporations to make business with the EU. The European Commission has the sole right of initiative and to propose new agreements, which she negotiates on behalf of member state.[3] This economic presence combined with its virility in external political economy makes the EU the "world champion of regulations"[4].

Next to many developing and industrializing countries, also most

---

[2] By comparison, the United States (USA) is the top trading partner for a little over 20 countries, with less openness to developing countries.

[3] Sieglinde Gstöhl (2013), The European Union's Trade Policy, *Ritsumeikan International Affairs*, Vol.11, 1-22, p.7

[4] The Director of the European Council on Foreign Relations (ECFR) dubbed the EU "Regulierungsweltmeister"; Mark Leonhard (2016), Interdependenz als Waffe. Die EU muss die Zeichen der geo-ökonomischen Zeit anerkennen, *Internationale Politik*, March/April 2016, p.100.

multinational corporations of developed countries are dependent on their exports to the EU and making business in the EU, so they need to adapt to European standards and regulations as well. The EU claims it has transparent rules and regulations and a secure legal investment framework that is among the most open in the world. However, the EU has not only be able to use its market power to export its rules and regulations, the European Commission also intervenes directly in foreign markets. It blocked the merger of General Electric and Honeywell and enforced Microsoft to separate Windows from Windows Explorer in the USA. It also impeded US agrarian sector doing business in Africa and other global markets with genetically modified organisms. The Commission therefore is an influential force in global economic regulation and market order, which makes it a power in and through trade, as Meunier and Nicolaidis opined in 2006 in an article that contributed much to the enfolding debate of the EU as a global regulatory power.[5] However and very recently, the common notion that the EU is a trade power that is able to enforce its rules externally due to its market size has become challenged, especially since the rising role of emerging markets in international trade.[6]

Till around 2010 the literature assumed that the EU is a very powerful trade policy actor. A main power resource of the Union is its market size and relevance as export market for the rest of the world. Therefore, the EU's ability to offer or withhold market access is the most important expression of power.[7] In recent years, this assumption became more differentiated, since trade policy results have been mixed.

---

[5] Sophie Meunier, Kalypso Nicolaidis (2006), The European Union as a conflicted trade power, *Journal of European Public Policy*, 13/6, pp.906-925.

[6] Steven M. McGuire, Johan P. Lindeque (2010), The Diminishing Returns of Trade Policy in the European Union, *Journal of Common Market Studies*, Vol.48/5, pp.1329-1349.

[7] Alasdair R. Young (2011), The Rise (and Fall?) of the EU's Performance in the Multilateral Trading System, *European Integration*, Vol.33, No.6, 715-729, November 2011, p.717.

The limitations of EU's effectiveness in global standard setting are also witnessed by EU's recent trade strategy from December 2015. Ten years after the EU launched its "Global Europe"[8] trade strategy, the European Commission cannot be satisfied with the performance, effectiveness and results. The ineffectiveness was exemplified by the failed interregional plans of a trade agreement between the EU and the Association of South East Asian Nations (ASEAN) in 2008. Moreover, also EU's influence on global trade policy within the World Trade Organization (WTO) has been shrinking in recent years, even though the EU is the only consistent long-standing supporter of the multilateral trading regime.[9] Towards ASEAN and the WTO, the EU was unable to project and promote its most favoured policies (namely the Singapore issues and the deep trade agenda, see below) as well as its favoured strategies (inter-regionalism and multilateralism).

Overall, the context in which the EU negotiates has received more attention: that is, when and in which context does the EU export its regulations, and when and in which situations does it stem away from doing or even trying to do so? How the global level does corresponded with EU's trade policy aspirations? Four strategies of regulatory export of the EU have been figured out: regulatory export; first-mover-agenda setting, mutual recognition, and coalition-building.[10] According to Newman and Posner, the EU is not strongly promoting its rules when

---

[8] European Commission (2006), Global Europe. Competing in the World. A Contribution to the EU's Growth and Jobs Strategy, accessed April 14, 2016, http://trade.ec.europa.eu/doclib/docs/2006/october/tradoc_130376.pdf

[9] The EU's shrinking influence in recent years has been noticed by Nicholas C. Niggli, a WTO insider and trade negotiator for many years who was for instance responsible for the mediation between the People's Republic of China and Taiwan on Taiwan's membership of the WTO Government Procurement Agreement (GPA).

[10] Abraham L. Newman, Elliot Posner (2015), Putting the EU in its place: policy strategies and the global regulatory context, *Journal of European Public Policy*, 22/9, pp.1316-1335.

she fears they may be seen as too ambitious in target countries.[11] Even within Preferential Trade Agreements (PTA) and the four new agreed ones (these are Canada, Central America, Singapore, and South Korea) and the ongoing TTIP, the regulatory co-ordination has been very limited. The bargaining power of the EU depends on whether the EU can or can not exclude others from its market. For the EU's regulatory cooperation, four 'values' have been figured out: No co-ordination, equivalence, convergence, and harmonization (on EU standards or international standards). In case the EU has no own standards or policies in a given field yet, and when she lacks internal cohesiveness, an equally strong partner will forward its policies easier. First-mover advantages then are on the side of the innovator. Therefore, assumptions of EU-USA negotiation results with regard to global power projection can be these: Those standards that are lower and more innovative (or "new") have a better chance for "uploading" to a global level than those standards that are perceived as higher and that have been negotiated since many years without resounding success.

Recent research suggests that the EU not always seeks to export its rules. The EU often advances progressive positions that are less extreme than its own single market rules to increase the likelihood of an agreement (especially when market exclusion is not possible). The EU will not demand insisting on harmonization on its own terms, if adjustment costs are so high that it might bring an agreement to fail that brings other benefits.[12] This is apparently the case with the EU's 'new generation' preferential trade agreements. The EU regulatory power resources are greatest when co-operation takes place through bargaining

---

[11] Alasdair Young (2015), Liberalizing trade, not exporting rules: the limits to regulatory co-ordination in the EU's 'new generation' preferential trade agreements, *Journal of European Public Policy*, 22/9, pp.1253-1275.

[12] Alasdair. R. Young (2015), The European Union as a global regulator? Context and comparison, *Journal of European Public Policy*, 22/9, p.1236.

and foreign firms or products can be excluded from the EU's market. When institutional density at global level is low, the EU is able to strongly influence global standards.

The EU has been more focusing on liberalizing trade in recent years than actually exporting its rules. Regulatory co-ordination with third partners has also been very limited in the very recent 'new generation' trade agreements, notably those with Canada, Central America, Singapore and South Korea.[13] Towards China, a completely different benchmark, Smith (2014) came to the conclusion that EU's economic diplomacy results were very limited.[14]

The EU's influence in FTA's seems most limited with respect to its peer, the United States. Context matters, not only mere power resources. In the FTA's with Canada, Central America, Singapore and South Korea, the EU has not really tried to export its regulations and has stronger focused on the equivalence of different rules or convergence based on international standards, not European standards.[15] When, however, European standards are 'too high' for the global level and when it is difficult to find global allies, for instance in situations when a great power like USA is against it, then there is only very limited chance for the EU to set global standards.

Still, the dominant common largest intersection for a bilateral trade deal is its global potential both EU and USA regularly emphasized. Both sides want to strengthen the multilateral trading system by using each other's leverage and for the promotion of new global rules.[16] Material

---

[13] Ibid.

[14] Michael Smith (2014), EU-China relations and the limits of economic diplomacy, *Asia Europe Journal*, 12/1-2, pp.35-48.

[15] Alasdair R. Young, 2015, supra note 11, pp.1253-1275.

[16] In 2013 the European Trade Commissioner Karel de Gucht said that "*this negotiation will set the standard – not only for our future bilateral trade and investment, including regulatory issues, but also for the development of global trade rules*", http://europa.eu/

Table 1: The EU's power in trade negotiations

High	Low
When it bargains with individual countries	When it negotiates with a group of actors that are strongly against EU's policies
When threat of exclusion from a market is possible	When threat of exclusion from market is not an option
When institutional density at global level is low (first-mover advantages?)	When density of standards at global level is already very high (no first mover advantages)
When institutional density at global level is low (first-mover advantages?)	When standards are too ambitious for global implementation
When it negotiates with weak countries	When it negotiates with equally strong countries
When internal cohesion is high (like on sanctions, anti-dumping policies)	When internal cohesion is low

interests matter, but geo-economic interests are more important.

When density of regulatory institutions at global level is rather low, promotion of global standards is easier. When there is no international organ and no active regulatory framework, than it is easier to project norms at global level. This may be the case for so-called modern 21st

rapid/press-release_SPEECH-13-147_en.htm (accessed 25 February 2016); The US President Barrack Obama opined concurrent:"*[W]e can achieve the kind of high-standard, comprehensive agreement that the global trading system is looking to us to develop [....]. And I believe we can forge an economic alliance as strong as our diplomatic and security alliances -- which, of course, have been the most powerful in history. ... And, by doing that, we can also strengthen the multilateral trading system.*" accessed February 25, 2016, https://www. whitehouse.gov/photos-and-video/video/2013/06/17/president-obama-makes-statement-transatlantic-trade-and-investment#transcript

century standards, where one can expect low global regulatory density. EU's external effort to promote openness 'the EU way' is more about replication than domination. The EU's power relies less on getting others to do what they would not do otherwise (classic definition of power) than on getting others to do what they otherwise would not do.[17] Neoliberal policies can be seen as a global minimum standard of regulation in many cases; power resources alone cannot explain outcome.

III. TTIP and EU's power to project global standards

Not only EU's, but also the leadership of the USA in trade policy has been challenged since the early 2000s.[18] Asia has overtaken the EU as the largest US export destination. However, trade conflicts with China have intensified in recent years. Priorities in EU's and US trade policy therefore have been modified since then (Table 2). The USA is top trading partner for the EU with a combined trade volume of half a trillion € in 2014. The USA is the EU's top export destination with more than 300 billion € in 2014. Only China exports more to the EU. US investment in the EU is three times higher than in all of Asia. EU investment in the US is around eight times the amount of EU investment in India and China together. Since the EU is slower recovering from economic crisis than the USA, the US market is of growing importance for the EU exporters. In 2015, the USA replaced France for the first time in decades and became the biggest export destination and trading partner for Germany (114 billion Euros compared to 106 billion Euros) and China.

What can be expected by EU-USA coordinated standards, on

---

[17] Meunier, Nicolaidis, op. cit., 2006, p.912.

[18] Alasdair Young, John Peterson (2006), The EU and the new trade politics, *Journal of European Public Policy*, pp.795-814.

which level will they meet in average when assuming that both actors are roughly the same size and the same powerful? In general, the actor with a more innovative approach, that is, so-called 21st century trade policies (supply chains policies, rules of origin, geographic indicators, e-commerce, data policy, state-operated enterprises), could stem more influence, since the institutional density at global level will be limited.

Table 2: Priorities in Trade Policy on "Global Standards": USA and EU compared

	USA (21st century agreements)	**EU ('deep trade agenda')**
Normative goals	Social standards and working conditions following societal pressure and negative consequences of NAFTA on US labour market	('managed globalisation' 1999-2003): human rights, social standards, environmental protection; revived by Lisbon Treaty (1999) and following protests against TTIP, consumer protection and "precautionary principle", "transparency"
Commercial goals	E-Commerce, State-Operated Enterprises, Supply-Chain-Policies and Rules of Origin, IPR, "scientific-based" consumer protection (mostly "innovative" politicies)	Singapore issues: public procurement, investment policy, competition policy (mostly "non-innovative" policies), access to raw materials
Defensive, strategic goals	Protection of neoliberal globalisation: anti-dumping, sanction policy, Investor-State Disputes, competition policy	Protection of neoliberal globalisation, cooperation on sanctions, anti-dumping

1. Comparison of trade power

Market size and assessment of power is not the only variable to assess who is more powerful and able to enforce its goals, especially in a game of two equals like USA and EU. The material comparison of EU and USA and the estimation about power in bilateral trade negotiations reveals more or less a draw. The EU has a slightly bigger economy than the USA. Both signed many FTA's before, although most partner countries are not big economies. Most notable, except the agreements both signed in their immediate neighbourhood, are the agreements with Korea and Singapore both sides settled. The USA has an advantage since it signed an agreement with a diverse group of Nations in the Transpacific Partnership Agreement (TPP), which still needs to be ratified by the US Congress. The by far largest bias in a comparison is the trade deficit the USA has with the EU. In 2015, it reached a record high of 153 billion US$. The deficit gives the USA an argument at hand to demand more concessions by the EU. Table 3 below compares the EU and USA at a glance with respect to their economies and bilateral trade.

With TTIP in place (and partly already during the negotiations during the last three years), the EU's at times sympathetic soft power may vanish and pave way to a more neoliberal US-styled way where corporate interests stay in the centre.

Why did the EU change its multilateral emphasis towards a bilateral one? Between the mid-1990ies and the early 2000's, the EU was the only strong promoter of a new multilateral WTO-round which led to the Doha Development Round. However, the hesitating USA fortified its trade policy orientation towards bilateralism at least since 2002-3. In 2003 at the ministerial meeting of the WTO the EU dropped its insistence on a 'deep trade agenda' with the so-called Singapore issues (transparent rules on investment, public procurement, and competition policy) as well as environmental protection and core labour standards.

Table 3: The EU and USA as trade powers in comparison

	EU	USA
Gross Domestic Product	18,495 trillion US$ (2014) (EU Commission)	17,937,8 trillion US$ (2015) (statista)
Population (mill.)	506	318
Imports from USA/ Imports from EU (2015, United States Census Bureau)	272,687 billion US$	426,005.6 billion US$
Trade volume (goods and services) in million US$ (WTO statistics 2014)	5 172 367 (~5 trillion US$)	6 233 791 (~6 trillion US$)
Active FTA's	(33) mostly in EU neighbourhood and Mediterranean area (Arabian countries, Israel), Mexico, Turkey (Customs Union)	(20) Australia, Bahrain, Canada, Chile, Colombia, Costa Rica, Dominican Republic El Salvador, Guatemala Honduras, Israel, Jordan Korea, Mexico, Morocco, Nicaragua, Oman, Panama, Peru, Singapore
Pending FTA's	Canada, Singapore	Transpacific Partnership (TPP)
FTA's in negotiation	Transatlantic Trade and Investment Partnership (TIPP)	Transatlantic Trade and Investment Partnership (TIPP)

With the new EU trade strategy "Global Europe"[19] the EU wanted to answer US' bilateral approach as well as the rise of China and other emerging markets. It goes without saying that the EU and the USA are used to negotiate on various issues on bilateral trade since decades and also within an increasingly institutionalised setting, yet it was not before the middle of the last decade, that both sides started to reason on a concrete bilateral trade agreement. Aggarval and Fogarty yet in 2005 stressed that "there is little strategic reason for the creation of a transatlantic free trade area, whether under current conditions or in the foreseeable future".[20] While the EU championed multilateralism for a long time, it has blanketed the world with bilateral trade agreements (now 33 at least, depending on how one counts them). The EU has used its huge market as a bargaining chip to obtain changes in the domestic policies of its trading partners, from labour standards to human rights "to shape new patterns of global governance"[21]. However, ten years later, the literature is not optimistic or sobered about these achievements in reality. Before 2006, the EU had a stronger normative content in its trade policy, with the 'Global Europe' strategy it became more mercantilist pursuing economic foreign policy objectives.[22]

At global level, the EU's involvement in multilateral bargaining was always shaped by its relationship to the USA. But the emergence of the new trading partners that were hostile to the EU's agenda and the extension of its rule-based system (at foremost Brazil, India, and

---

[19] European Commission (2006), Global Europe. Competing in the World. A Contribution to the EU's Growth and Jobs Strategy, accessed April 14, 2016, http://trade. ec.europa.eu/doclib/docs/2006/october/tradoc_130376.pdf

[20] Aggarval, Vinod K., Fogarty, Edward (2005), The Limits of Interregionalism: The EU and North America, *European Integration*, Vol.27, No.3, pp.327-346.

[21] Sophie Meunier, Kalypso Nicolaidis (2006), The European Union as a conflicted trade power, *Journal of European Public Policy* 13/6, p.907.

[22] Sophie Meunier (2007), Managing Globalization? The EU in International Trade Negotiations, *Journal of Common Market Studies*, 45/4, pp.905-926.

China) have gradually eroded EU's ambition to shape the multilateral trading system in the WTO system.[23] The failed promotion of EU priorities in multilateral trade policy while being the largest trade actor globally leads to the question whether EU standards were too high for a globalising political economy. Since bilateral developments of EU-US economic relations are not the main reason for TTIP negotiations, a major incentive may lie in EU's problematic trade policy performance and the development of the external environment in recent years. TTIP is therefore already a result of a transformed EU trade policy.

2.   Discussion of EU and US standards at global level

What have been the most important goals of EU's trade policy since the late 1990ies? Most importantly, The EU wishes to export it so-called 'deep trade agenda' with regulatory effect beyond borders, namely competition policy, environmental and labour standards, investment rules, sanitary and phytosanitary standards, rules on public procurement, protection of intellectual property rights, and some other policies. Since 1995, EU includes also human rights clauses in all accords. There are now such 120 treaties. The EU may reduce development aid when a government annihilates civil activists. However, even the EU could do so, it practically never applies such measures. For the USA the same holds true. Both have included human rights clauses with their trade agreements towards Columbia, but they both remained unused.[24] Whether the EU, as Meunier/Nikolaidies stated in 2006, really used trade to achieve non-trade objectives, is questionable from today's perspective.[25] Ten years later and with an obligation within the Lisbon Treaty to attach human rights

---

[23] Alasdair Young (2011), The Rise (and Fall?) of the EU's Performance in the Multilateral Trading System, *European Integration*, Vol.33/6, 715-729, p.716.

[24] Petra Pinzler, TTIP ist keine Wundertüte. Warum sich Hoffnungen und Wünsche nicht realisieren werden, Internationale Politik, März/April 2016, p.114.

[25] Meunier/Nikolaidis, op. cit., 2006, p.912.

the greatest importance, the results look bleach.

The EU has not achieved any or much progress with its Singapore issues. In addition, the EU's approach is not pure neoliberal, but also can be seen as "progressive" (like the so-called 'managed-globalisation' approach during the protectionist Pascal Lamy era as EU Trade Commissioner, including environmental protection, labour protections, precautionary principle and consumer protection, among others). Such "socialist-progressive" policies are very difficult to negotiate with the USA, yet more difficult it is at global level.

The negotiations on a TTIP therefore could be to a large extent explained by a changed role and transformed influence (or the perception thereof) of the EU in trade negotiations.

No other bilateral trade partners fought more conflicts than the USA and Europe over decades. The pattern started with the 'chicken war' of 1963-4, in which USA demanded GATT (General Agreement on Tariffs and Trade, the predecessor of WTO) invoked compensation for loss of market share following the establishment of the customs union. Bitterly contested were also conflict cases over tuna, subsidized steel exports, wheat, canned fruit, bananas, oilseed, bovine growth hormones and nowadays chlorine chicken and dispute settlement. Both were the most enthusiastic users of the WTO dispute settlement, mostly against each other over many years. This has changed in recent years, and China is getting more often in the focus of EU and USA together, like seen with the conflicts of China's rare earth export restrictions, solar subsidies, enforced IPR transfers and discriminating investment policies. The external environment may be the main reason why both sides now try to put their decades' long disputes aside or at least try to deal with them in a yet more formalised way in future.

21st century trade agreements have a different content than what the EU previously promoted globally. The USA just concluded the Transpacific Trade Partnership (TTP), which, when ratified in the

Parliaments, may become the world's largest free trade area (TTIP not counted here). Since the US government is strong under pressure from civil society, the Congress may demand stronger human rights and environment protection in future trade agreements, which would support a common transatlantic normative approach.[26] TPP excludes the People's Republic of China (China), but puts the EU in defence, which failed to negotiate a deep EU regulatory style interregional agreement with the ASEAN in 2008. Now, with the TTIP under negotiation, the USA is in a comfortable position to negotiate and promote a US regulatory style globally, that may exploit the EU as a stepping stone for its own trade policy goals.[27] Digital trade, localization barriers to trade in the digital environment, and state-owned enterprises are said to be emerging "21st century" issues. These 21st century issues are included in the TPP and comprise regulatory coherence, state-owned enterprises, e-commerce and data transfer, competitiveness and supply chains. Competition policies, trade remedies (that is, trade defense measures), intellectual property rights, rules of origin and foreign investment were also central TPP themes. These policies, included in TIPP, would mean a dominance of global standard setting favoring US goals for years to come.

With regard to financial services regulation, the EU Commission proposed for regulatory co-ordination within TIPP and for mutual reliance, equivalence and substituted compliance, rather than any form of compliance. The EU, after resistance by the US to open that chapter, has not sought to export its prudential supervision rules. In data protection, the EU has sought actively to exclude this topic, since it feared there would be downward pressure from USA rules on European standards.

---

[26] Reinhard Biedermann, The Conflicts between the Obama Administration and Congress on the Trans-Pacific Partnership Agreement, *Tamkang Journal of International Affairs*, 26/4, pp.43-86.

[27] Davies, Peter (2013), Trade secrets: Will an EU-US treaty enable US big business to gain a foothold? *British Medical Journal*, Vol. 346, Issue 7911, pp.16-18.

Rather, convergence is based overwhelmingly on international standards. Within the main fields of regulatory co-ordination the EU and USA have no convergence in TIPP (competition policy, data protection, environment, labour) limited (food), or reciprocal equivalence (vehicles, financial services). The EU's export of data protection standards is very limited. In case global standards are lower than US standards, and US standards are lower than EU standards, the EU may try to avoid the negotiations or at least try to agree on slightly higher common standards with the USA to "upload" them on global level commonly to raise global standards.

Obviously, it was easier for the USA to implement such 21st century trade policies within an equally diverse framework of TPP, while the EU-ASEAN trade negotiations failed years before. Public procurement was seen as a main reason why the negotiations failed. Again, public procurement is also on top of EU's TTIP goals.[28] The EU´s standards are high and demanding, whereas the US policies enjoy not only first mover advantages more often, but also a common denominator on a neoliberal footing. A common management of standards could therefore provide "high enough" standards in cases where the EU can not enforce its own rules.

IV The transformative power of TTIP on global standard setting

Firstly, the EU re-emphasizes normative policies within TTIP from the 'managed globalisation' era of the centre-left governments in EU in the late 1990ies. Regarding these policies, the USA is EU's natural partner and vice versa. The TTIP negotiations already changed the way how

---

[28] European Commission, Brussels, 22-26 February 2016, The Twelfth Round of Negotiations for the Transatlantic Trade and Investment Partnership (TTIP), Public Report – March. 1-17.

the EU conducts its trade policy. In September 2015 the EU published its new trade strategy (see above). Normative policies that have been disregarded since 2006 in EU's trade policy have been reemphasized.

Secondly, the transformative power of EU's trade strategy following the rise of China. The literature assumes that China is mostly a 'good' WTO member that implemented the rules well. However, most WTO members are developing countries and mostly abide by the rules, despite a much less effective state bureaucracy than China can rely on. A WTO membership is much less demanding than being an EU member. The most relevant WTO policies from US and EU perspective are strategically disregarded by China (IPR, investment, subsidies, public procurement, etc.). However, these policies are lax within the WTO (also because of China and its insistence being a developing country). TTIP may contribute to change this, and it could give more leverage to EU's role as regulatory actor in fields where China disregards basic WTO principles like on investment.

1. *Normative Policies*

Article 21 of the Treaty of Lisbon mandates the EU to foster its values in its external relations (democracy, rule of law, social rights, gender, equality, etc.). FTA's are accompanied by a Political Cooperation Agreement (PCA) which links core values to trade through the 'standard clause', whereby under certain circumstances , human rights' abuses can trigger a suspension of trade preferences. However, Garcia and Masselot (2015) in their study revealed that the EU is unsuccessful in pushing forward social issues in its FTAs because EU's Asian partner resists the legalistic approach of the EU.[29] It will be seen whether a TTIP can strengthen the West's human rights policies. Next to external

---

[29] Maria Garcia, Annick Masselot (2015), EU-Asia Free Trade Agreements as tools for social norm/legislation transfer, *Asia Europe Journal*, 13/3, pp.241-252.

norms referring to 'output legitimacy', also 'input legitimacy' has been transformed.

In its new trade strategy, the EU has a more transparent trade and investment policy to settle protests and anger at home. The EU pledges to extend the "TTIP transparency initiative" to all the EU trade negotiations. It also publishes negotiating texts on the Commission's website. The EU Commission also wants to base its trade and investment policies on values (however serious this is meant). The EU wants to

- Safeguard EU regulatory protection and lead the reform investment policy globally.
- Expand measures to support sustainable development, fair and ethical trade and human rights, including by ensuring effective implementation of related FTA provisions and the Generalised Scheme of Preferences.
- Include anti-corruption rules in future trade agreements.

However, not only China, also India as the other Asian giant and democratic country hesitates to adopt the EU's preferred model for liberalization, like in the case of public procurement. Neither is India interested to accept normative or human rights standards within trade agreements.[30] Normative standards are still interpreted as protectionism by many non-Western countries.

2. *Commercial Policies*

The European Union wants to shape globalisation by a new programme of negotiations that can be interpreted as an answer on USA's agreed TTP and the growing assertiveness of China in trade policy. The EU wants

---

[30] Jan Orbie, Sangeeta Khorana (2015), Normative versus market power Europe? The EU-India trade agreement, 13/3, pp.253-264.

to reenergise multilateral negotiations and design an "open approach to bilateral and regional agreements, including TTIP". EU's presence in Asia and Pacific shall be strenghtened. The EU wants to set "ambitious objectives with China" and request a mandate (from the European Council) for FTA negotiations with Australia and New Zealand, and ASEAN FTA negotiations with the Philippines and Indonesia, "when appropriate". Also towards other regions like Africa within the Economic Partnership Agreements (EPA) and the African Union as well as regarding other existing agreements with Turkey, Mexico, and Chile the EU wants to "modernise" the existing agreements.

New topics will include raw materials access, especially since the EU has set-up an own raw materials diplomacy since 2008 and operationalised since very recently. The Chinese rare earth policies acted as a catalyst to a stronger raw materials policy of the EU.[31] The EU modernised its trade policy content (21st century agreements similar to the US and TPP). It wants "a more effective policy" (read: the old one was not effective) that "tackles new economic realities and lives up to its promises by

- Updating trade policy to take account of the new economic realities such as global value chains, the digital economy and the importance of services.
- Supporting mobility of experts, senior managers, and service providers.
- Setting up an enhanced partnership with the Member States, the European Parliament and stakeholders to implement trade and investment agreements better.

---

[31] Reinhard Biedermann (2016), The EU's Raw Materials Diplomacy. Market Access and Development? European Foreign Affairs Review, 21/1.

- Including effective SME provisions in future trade agreements."[32]

Regarding investment policies it was a goal since the 'deep trade agenda' to not only protect investment, but also ensure that the governments of host countries can regulate the activities of investors and noting the need to address inverstors' responsibilities. The EU has reemphasized this policy also in its latest trade strategy. The fears of European societies, especially the German society (Germany even invented investment protection in the 1960ies and has concluded the most BITs globally) are very high and may give a death blow to the TTIP negotiations if the US do not accept public arbitration.

3. Economic NATO in defence of neoliberal globalisation

In 2006, Der Spiegel author Gabor Steingart perceived a transatlantic trade deal as economic NATO that would bring Europe and the USA closer again. It could also serve as an answer on the challenge of the rise of Asia with its focus on materialism and collectivism.[33] Mostly, the expression "economic NATO" has been used by US policymakers, like by the then secretary of state Hillary Clinton.[34] Strong support for a trade agreement since years comes from Germany, whose chancellor Merkel supports a deal, which is said to be one of her favourite political projects, at least since 2006, when Germany held the EU presidency. Some observers forecast a backlash in emerging markets against a TTIP "going" global. Charles A. Kupchan, Georgetown University, warned that

---

[32] European Commission- Fact Sheet. Q&A on 'Trade for All', the Commission's new trade and investment strategy, accessed April 14, 2016, http://europa.eu/rapid/press-release_MEMO-15-5807_en.htm, 15 October 2015

[33] Steingart, Gabor (2006), A NATO for the World Economy. An Argument for a Trans-Atlantic Free-Trade Zone, 20.10.2006.

[34] Clingendael Policy Brief (2013), The Geopolitics of TTIP, *Clingendael Institute*, No.23, October, accessed April 14, 2016, http://www.clingendael.nl/sites/default/files/The%20 Geopolitics%20of%20TTIP%20-%20Clingendael%20Policy%20Brief.pdf

a TTIP has the potential to widen the split between the West and these countries. Sun Zhenyu from China's trade ministry wrote that TTIP and TPP will impede that China and other emerging markets co-write future international rules, and they will enforce them to adapt to these rules: "But no-one will stop China's rise", as he expressed. If TTIP and TPP threaten Russia and China, then other countries like Brazil, India or Indonesia may be affected as well, as Pinzler wrote.[35] Xiaotang et al. (2014) wrote that China would become increasingly concerned about the potential trade diversion effects and the possible G2 domination by the EU and the US in terms of rule-making power in world trade.[36] However, De Ville's and Siles-Bruegge's (2015) TTIP elaborations result in doubts that a negotiated TTIP will establish new "gold standard" trading rules for the rest of the world.[37]

In Germany and also within the EU the thinking on global trade and particularly China began to change in 2005 and 2006. During the second half of the 2000s, almost any Commission publication related to China began with the sentence "China is the single most important challenge for EU trade policy."[38] The EU published a long list of complaints directed against China. Although EU officials do not talk on "economic NATO", the trade directorate may have the same in mind. The EU demands from China:

- Economic openness
- Market economy reform

[35] Petra Pinzler, op. cit., p.116.

[36] Zhang Xiaotang, Zhang Ping, Yang Xiaoyan (2014), The EU's New FTA Adventures and Their Implications for China, *Journal of World Trade*, 48/3, pp.525-552.

[37] Ferdi de Ville, Gabriel Sildes-Bruegge, TTIP: The Truth about the Transatlantic Trade and Investment Partnership, Polity, 2015, p.160.

[38] European Commission, External Trade, Competition and Partnership; a Policy for EU-China Trade Investment. Executive Summary, accessed April 12, 2016, http://trade.ec.europa.eu/doclib/docs/2006/november/tradoc_131235.pdf

- Legal protection for foreign companies
- Enforcement of protection
- Reject anti-competitive trading practices and policies
- End of enforced technology transfers for European investors
- Unfair subsidisation
- To meet WTO obligations
- Liberalise access to its goods, services, investment, public procurement markets

Of growing concern in Europe is outgoing FDI from China, particular the investments of state-led corporations. Chinese companies that invest in Europe are mostly state corporations that comprise around 70 per cent of Chinese FDI, according to a study of the Merics China Research Institute in Berlin.[39] These companies are especially looking for key industries like in the car sector (Kiekert), water and environment technology (Bilfinger, EEW), or specialised machine industry (Putzmeister, Schwing).[40]

There are bureaucratic and geo-economic reasons why the EU Commission was so keen to put the chapter on Bilateral Investment Treaties in TTIP. Firstly, it is a new competence since the Treaty of Lisbon in 2009. The EU Commission simply raises its own legitimacy and power in negotiating on investments with the USA, although economically it is without any economic benefit for the EU and its societies, but may even be harmful and costly. Secondly, a deal with the USA on investments raises the pressure on China to follow and accept investment rules both

---

[39] Thilo Hanemann, Mikko Huotari (2015), Chinese FDI in Europe and Germany. Preparing for a New Era of Chinese Capital. A Report by the Mercator Institute for China Studies and Rhodium Group, June, pp.1-56.

[40] Ulrich Friese und Oliver Schmale, "Der Chef kommt jetzt aus China," Frankfurter Allgemeiner, accessed April 9, 2016, http://www.faz.net/aktuell/beruf-chance/arbeitswelt/mittelstand-der-chef-kommt-jetzt-aus-china-14154240.html.

transatlantic actors have negotiated before. This on the other hand, would justify a deal, since China has for long been exploiting the liberal investment regimes of the West, while demanding joint ventures on the home market, against basic WTO standards. The same argument holds true for public procurement. While China may benefit from the collusive public procurement markets in Central Europe and Asia, especially ASEAN, with its own collusive strategies, a common transatlantic deal on public procurement would help create a level playing field that would benefit the most competitive corporations and therefore provide prosperity gains to societies on the Eurasian continent. The huge plans of China for new silk roads to connect Europe with China should be seen in this context as well.

V. Conclusion

The TTIP negotiations between the EU and USA are firstly a result of the EU's mixed performance of its trade policy in the recent years, but have itself already transformed EU's trade policy as well. The EU's trade policy was not very effective in the recent decade. It was neither able to project its trade policy goal globally effectively, nor was it able to agree ambitious trade agreements, with Korea and Singapore being the only exemptions. However, even towards these most advanced Asian Nations, the literature suggests a rather lax approach regarding EU's proclaimed goals, even regarding the huge power bias measured in economic size between the EU and the two mentioned developed Asian players that would suggest otherwise.

Without any doubt, strategic goals have become more important in EU's trade policy, especially defensive instruments. External pressure on the EU will rise, and its soft power image may suffer. However, since EU's soft power in trade regulation was over assessed in recent decades, it is time to reassess the EU's trade policy and to become more realistic about the goals the EU can achieve in global trade policy. The TTIP transformed EU's global trade policy strategy towards more realistic, modern goals where global regulatory density is rather low. However, also normative goals ('managed globalisation' from 1999 to 2003) are "rediscovered". They always played a role in EU's trade policy, but were never effectively implemented. Protectionism from the left and right political wings is on the rise in USA and the EU. Therefore such normative, protectionist policies will be stronger emphasized in future.

Geo-economic goals in TTIP negotiations loom large, since the current neoliberal globalisation is challenged in distinct fields, especially by China. Therefore, defensive policies will become yet more important in EU's trade policy, while too ambitious European regulatory single market policies will become less important. Public procurement and the investment negotiations between the EU and the USA need to be seen also in context with China's rise and growing investment in foreign markets. Global investment and procurement rules may also help regulate China's "One Belt, One Road"- Initiative of large infrastructural investments on the Eurasian continent.

國家圖書館出版品預行編目 (CIP) 資料

歐盟貿易政策新趨勢 / 陳麗娟主編 . -- 一版 . --
　新北市 : 淡大出版中心 , 2016.07
　　面 ；　公分
　部分內容為英文
　ISBN 978-986-5608-27-9(平裝)

　1. 歐洲聯盟 2. 貿易政策

558.1　　　　　　　　　　　　　105012059

叢書編號 PS012

歐盟貿易政策新趨勢 *The New Trend of the EU Trade Policy*

著　　者　陳麗娟　主編

社　　長　林信成
總 編 輯　吳秋霞
行政編輯　張瑜倫
行銷企劃　陳卉綺
內文排版　張明蕙
封面設計　斐類設計工作室

發 行 人　張家宜
出 版 者　淡江大學出版中心
　　　　　地址：25137 新北市淡水區英專路 151 號
　　　　　電話：02-86318661/ 傳真：02-86318660
出版日期　2016 年 8 月 一版一刷
定　　價　300 元

總 經 銷　紅螞蟻圖書有限公司
展 售 處　淡江大學出版中心
　　　　　地址：新北市 25137 淡水區英專路 151 號海博館 1 樓
　　　　　電話：02-86318661　　傳真：02-86318660
　　　　　淡江大學─驚聲書城
　　　　　地址：新北市淡水區英專路 151 號商管大樓 3 樓